Reflections on First and Second Peter

Ray Ruppert

Reflections on First and Second Peter

Tex Ware
Everett, WA

Scripture references marked (KJV) are taken from the Holy Bible, King James Version.

The Bible text designated (NIV®) is Scripture taken from the Holy Bible, NEW INTERNATIONAL VERSION®, NIV® Copyright © 1973, 1978, 1984 by Biblica, Inc.® Used by permission. All rights reserved worldwide.

Scripture references marked (NASB) are taken from the New American Standard Bible, © 1960, 1963, 1968, 1971, 1972, 1973, 1975, 1977 by The Lockman Foundation. Used by permission.

Scripture quotations marked (NLT) are taken from the Holy Bible, New Living Translation, copyright 1996, 2004. Used by permission of Tyndale House Publishers, Inc., Wheaton, Illinois 60189. All rights reserved.

The Bible text designated (RSV) is from the REVISED STANDARD VERSION OF THE BIBLE, Copyright © 1946, 1952, 1971 by the Division of Christian Education of the National Council of the Churches of Christ in the USA, and is used by permission.

The Bible text designated (TLB) is from THE LIVING BIBLE, copyright © 1971. Used by permission of Tyndale House Publishers, Inc., Wheaton, IL 60189. All rights reserved.

Greek and Hebrew definitions are from Biblesoft's New Exhaustive Strong's Numbers and Concordance with Expanded Greek-Hebrew Dictionary. Copyright © 1994, 2003, 2006 Biblesoft, Inc. and International Bible Translators, Inc. unless otherwise noted.

ISBN-13: 978-1-935500-47-6
ISBN-10: 1935500473
Library of Congress Control Number: 2011900653

To: The Lord Jesus Christ
May His persecuted Church find hope and perseverance.
To: Saul Masih and those holding up the light of the Gospel in
closed countries.

Table of Contents

Foreword

I originally wrote this work as a series of blogs. My first goal was to get deeper into the Word than just doing a daily reading and then walking away, not even remembering what I've read. Much of this is written in the first person as I wanted to write what I learned for my life, not necessarily what I think God is saying to others. Pardon me when I lapse into academic style or slip out of the first person.

My secondary goal was to provide some encouragement to others who might read the posts or this book. I picked 1st and 2nd Peter because there is a lot in here about suffering as Christians, whether it is a result of persecution or simply living in a fallen world. Hopefully, this can help keep Christians from panicking when something goes wrong in their lives.

It was not my goal to point fingers or kick anyone in his spiritual behind. However, some passages are there for that very reason. I hope I have handled these appropriately. I pray that in these situations, eyes will be opened, repentance undertaken, and even salvation for people who may read this and discover that they are wandering from the Christian path or may never been on it in the first place.

First Peter – Chapter One

1 Peter 1:1-2

Peter, an apostle of Jesus Christ, To God's elect, strangers in the world, scattered throughout Pontus, Galatia, Cappadocia, Asia and Bithynia, who have been chosen according to the foreknowledge of God the Father, through the sanctifying work of the Spirit, for obedience to Jesus Christ and sprinkling by his blood: Grace and peace be yours in abundance. (NIV®)

Ok, I'm not sure that I really want to start out with these verses; verses about election! Do I really want to comment on verses that have divided Christians for centuries? Well, if I want to be true to the Word, I can't skip over them and not study them. I certainly don't want to offend someone with what I believe God is teaching me, but I don't want to miss a blessing from God because I'm afraid to state clearly what I believe the Word is saying. I'll try to side with Paul as he stated in Galatians 1:10: *Am I now trying to win the approval of men, or of God? Or am I trying to please men? If I were still trying to please men, I would not be a servant of Christ.* (NIV®)

With all that out of the way, I'll actually start commenting on the verses. As I look at the (NIV®), the first words that stand out are elect, strangers, scattered, and chosen. I double-checked with NASB and an interlinear Bible to make sure the words are really there in the original Greek.

Elect or chosen. The Greek is *eklektos* (ek-lek-tos'); select; by implication, favorite: KJV – chosen, elect. Rather than reiterate what hundreds or thousands have had to say about election, I simple want to understand what God is saying to me and to anyone who knows Jesus. I'm His favorite. I'm not His last pick for choosing sides. I may not have come over the first time He called but out of that line up of humanity, He selected me. What can I say except, "Thank you, Jesus." I certainly can't say that I deserved it or earned His calling. There was nothing I did or will do that caused Him to say He wanted me. The word that goes with this selection is foreknowledge.

The Greek for foreknowledge is *prognosis* (prog'-no-sis). Guess what it means: forethought. Two things come to mind. God thought about me before I was even conceived. He knew me and wanted me to be His. This word is what we always hear regarding health issues. What is the prognosis? How is this disease, injury, or condition going to turn out? Being in sin is like a disease and the ultimate prognosis is death and eternal condemnation. But God's prognosis for me is eternal life with Him. It's good to know that the Person making the prognosis is the One who is capable of making it happen. See Psalm 139:1-18 for more about how God knows us.

Jeremiah 1:5 says, *"Before I formed you in the womb I knew you, before you were born I set you apart; I appointed you as a prophet to the nations."* (NIV®) Speaking to the prophet Jeremiah, God has a word for me too. He formed me, He sets me apart, and He appoints my function in life. If God is sovereign, then He is sovereign in all things and that includes my destiny. My pea-sized brain can't hope to comprehend how He can have total control and foreknowledge (He knows that some will not accept Him and others will) as well as give everyone the opportunity to know Him (John 3:16, Romans 10:9-13). I can only say along with Paul, "Who knows the mind of the Lord?" (Rom 11:34) His being is too much, too great for me to comprehend. I can only stand or fall down in awe.

Strangers or aliens (NASB). At first glance, you would think that Peter is addressing those who are aliens because they are now living in a country where they had to flee from persecution. However, Peter also speaks in 1 Peter 2:11 about being aliens and strangers regarding behavior. Paul explains in Ephesians 2:12 that we Gentiles were not citizens of Israel and therefore had no part in the promises of God. But through the blood of Jesus, we have been brought near to God. Again in Philippians 3:20 Paul clearly states we are citizens of heaven. The reason we are aliens is that our home country is not of this world. Our behavior and our customs should be different from those around us.

There are many people in the US (and other countries as well) who think that Christians are out to destroy the country. They believe we have a hidden agenda to overthrow it and make it a "Christian" nation. Part of that fear is based on the fact that we do behave differently. Personally, am I different enough to be identified as a stranger or alien? If not, then something is wrong. What do I need to change? I think I've been trying to blend in too much so that I won't be criticized. It gets back to that stuff I mentioned up above about wanting to please God rather than man. Lord, help me be an alien that pleases You.

I have been chosen and it is through the sanctifying work of the Holy Spirit. If anyone has seen the Stargate TV series, then you know about the Goa'uld. These are alien, snake-like creatures that use humans as hosts and take over. These are totally evil beings. On the other hand, there are also some of the same alien species that are good but are called the Tok'ra. I wonder how many people view Christians as Goa'uld (evil) because we have the Holy Spirit living in us. In one of the first TV episodes people are "chosen" to be hosts. If I knew nothing of our God and Jesus and had seen these TV shows, what would I think of people who say they have the Holy Spirit living in them? I would probably say they are possessed. Well, quite frankly, I am possessed! I have surrendered my body to someone who is outside of our physical domain. I have become a slave of God and the benefit is holiness and eternal life (Romans 6:22). This is really scary to people who want to do their own thing.

Then the Word in 1 Peter 1:2 also says that the purpose of my being chosen is obedience to Jesus and sprinkling by His blood. Whoa! What does that mean? Many verses in the Bible talk about sprinkling blood. The blood from animal sacrifices was used to cover sin and cleanse objects and people to make them acceptable to God. But in the New Testament, it is clear that Jesus willingly shed His blood once (instead of the many animal sacrifices) so that God would forgive our sins and accept us. Not only does His blood buy our redemption but it also clears our consciences. Hebrews 9:13-14: *The blood of goats and bulls and the ashes of a heifer sprinkled on those who are ceremonially unclean sanctify them so that they are outwardly clean. How much more, then, will the blood of Christ, who through the eternal Spirit offered himself unblemished to God, cleanse our consciences from acts that lead to death, so that we may serve the living God!* (NIV®)

It is understandable that this may freak people out who do not know Jesus. If I am truly following Jesus, then I act differently and talk about being sprinkled by His blood. I have a clear conscience and say I'm holy because of that. I'm called arrogant because I speak confidently of this, even though I'm not perfect.

Blessed be God – 1 Peter 1:3

Blessed be the God and Father of our Lord Jesus Christ, who according to His great mercy has caused us to be born again to a living hope through the resurrection of Jesus Christ from the dead. (NASB)

My first thought is that I could camp out on the first phrase for a long time, even the first word. I've never looked up the word blessed. It sounds good in this verse but what do I mean when I say God is blessed? In Hebrews 7:7 the writer says that the lesser is blessed by the greater. How can I bless God? The good old dictionary and the Greek cleared up the confusion for me. The dictionary[1] has several definitions and the one that fits in verse 3 is "worthy of adoration, reverence, or worship: the Blessed Trinity." Checking out the Greek, the word is *eulogetos* (yoo-log-ay-tos'); adorable.

Our God is adorable. If I adore my wife, and I do, is this the same adoration that I have for God? My wife is attractive, delightful and charming – a definition of adorable. Would I describe God that way? Yes and no. He is much more than that. Adorable is also being worthy to be adored. Knowing sign language helps because the same sign is used for adore and worship. From now on, when I see verses that say "Blessed be God" I will think of how worthy He is of worship. Worship is the reverent honor and homage paid to God. What is homage? A dictionary[2] definition is the formal public acknowledgment by which a feudal tenant or vassal declared himself to be the man or vassal of his lord, owing him fidelity and service. OK, now we're getting somewhere. I can only worship God when I belong to Him.

A vassal was essentially a slave. As a vassal of God, I am owned by Him and in worship I acknowledge that He has complete authority over me. A vassal was granted land in return for paying homage to the lord, a portion of the crops, and even military service. Isn't that the picture of a Christian? God gives me life, everything I have on this earth, and an inheritance in heaven. In return, I give back to Him

---

[1] American Heritage® Dictionary of the English Language
[2] Encarta® World English Dictionary [North American Edition] © & (P)2009 Microsoft Corporation.

myself, tithes and offerings, my service to spread His Word. Living the Christian life is often symbolized as warfare.

I'm glad that I picked the NASB for this verse since the NIV® says "Praise be to God…" I don't think I would have discovered the richness of the first four words otherwise. In many verses in the O.T. the NIV® uses "praise" where the NASB uses "bless." The NIV® is much more readable than the NASB, but that may be only because my vocabulary is limited. The NIV® is written to be more understandable at a lower reading level than the NASB.

The phrase, "God and Father of our Lord Jesus Christ" appears only four times in the Bible. (Romans 15:6, 2 Corinthians 1:3, Ephesians 1:3, and 1 Peter 1:3) I sometimes become messed up trying to think of God and Jesus. So what do I do? I go back to what I know for sure, that Jesus and God the Father are one. John 1:1 *In the beginning was the Word, and the Word was with God, and the Word was God.* (NASB) This has to be the clearest declaration of the deity of Jesus and the unity of God and Jesus. The next thing I do is think about what it means to say Jesus is our Lord. It goes back that vassal thing above. He owns me and I am His.

Do I worship Jesus in the same way that I worship God the Father? Yes! Absolutely! How do I know that it is OK to worship Jesus? Well, I'll start with what Jesus said. Matthew 4:10 *Then Jesus said to him, "Begone, Satan! For it is written, 'You shall worship the Lord your God, and serve Him only.'"* (NASB) Clearly, Jesus says by quoting the O.T. that we should only worship and serve God. John 9:38 *Then the man said, "Lord, I believe," and he worshiped him.* (NIV®) Of course you then need to read and see how Jesus responded to worship. Did Jesus rebuke the man for worshiping Him? Not at all, in fact He used the situation to point out to the Pharisees that they were spiritually blind. When Thomas first saw Jesus after His resurrection, he declared that Jesus was his Lord and God. John 20:28-29 *Thomas answered and said to Him, "My Lord and my God!" Jesus said to him, "Because you have seen Me, have you believed? Blessed are they who did not see, and yet believed."* (NASB) Did Jesus rebuke Thomas? Well, yes, but not for calling Jesus Lord and God, but because he had to see Jesus physically first. For us who have not seen Jesus in the flesh, we are blessed when we believe. This Greek word for blessed is not at all the same one that was used before.

This is *makarios* (mak-ar'-ee-os) which means happy. In just a few more verses I'll see why I should be happy.

One of the reasons that God is worthy of my worship is because of His great mercy. I just can't keep away from looking up the Greek since some versions use the word abundant instead of great. While abundant is much more descriptive of God's mercy, the Greek is *polus* (pol-oos') which means much or many or large, so great is probably more accurate. Now I'm off on a rabbit trail because *polus* sounds a lot like Palouse which is a huge, abundant wheat producing area in eastern Washington that extends into Idaho and Oregon. If you've ever driven through the area in the spring, it is a beautiful green and turns to gold when the wheat ripens later in the year. The origin of the word Palouse is debated but thought to come from French and has nothing to do with abundance or greatness but it should. God's abundant and great mercy is certainly shown by the provision we receive from this part of our nation.

The love of God, His mercy and grace can be seen in the O.T. as well as the N.T. However, to understand His mercy and grace I also have to understand that without it, I would be suffering His wrath. The following verses express His mercy, my guilt, and the consequences if I did not receive His mercy. Exodus 34:6-7 *Then the Lord passed by in front of him and proclaimed, "The Lord, the Lord God, compassionate and gracious, slow to anger, and abounding in lovingkindness and truth; who keeps lovingkindness for thousands, who forgives iniquity, transgression and sin; yet He will by no means leave the guilty unpunished, visiting the iniquity of fathers on the children and on the grandchildren to the third and fourth generations."* (NASB). My sin and rebellion against God will certainly have far-reaching consequences, not only on my eternal destiny but also upon my children and those of others. The people I vote for, the causes I embrace, my attitude toward nature, if not guided by God are sin and affect many generations.

The greatness of His mercy can be seen in Ephesians 2:4-5 *But because of his great love for us, God, who is rich in mercy, made us alive with Christ even when we were dead in transgressions — it is by grace you have been saved.* (NIV®) God has taken me out of the realm of the dead and given me life. Of course, before this happened, I thought I was alive, not realizing that my spirit was dead because of my sins. That's the biggest problem in presenting the Gospel to anyone, convincing a person that he or she is a sinner. My friend, Larry Kent, has written some tracts that help do this. They have been translated into many languages. Go to http:// www.on-tract.com to see them.

Now, back to the Bible. One last thing about God's mercy and love; it isn't like my concept of love. I generally love others because they are nice people and we get along with each other. These are people who are relatively decent toward others. However, can I say that I love my enemy or those who have insulted, maligned, or ignored me? Before becoming a Christian I was an enemy of God whether I knew it or not. Most of us would probably say we were not enemies of God. Unfortunately, the Bible says that when I love the stuff in the world which isn't aligned with God's plan and direction, I'm His enemy. James 4:4 *You adulterous people, don't you know that friendship with the world is hatred toward God? Anyone who chooses to be a friend of the world becomes an enemy of God.* (NIV®) So how great is God's mercy? This is how great it is: Romans 5:8 *But God demonstrates His own love toward us, in that while we were yet sinners, Christ died for us.* (NASB) How about that? Jesus died for me when I was His enemy.

Yes, God is worthy of worship – blessed – because of His great mercy.

New Birth – 1 Peter 1:3

Blessed be the God and Father of our Lord Jesus Christ, who according to His great mercy has caused us to be born again to a living hope through the resurrection of Jesus Christ from the dead. (NASB)

"Are you one of those born again Christians?" I was asked. I answered yes. Why did I say that I was born again? Verse 3 says that God has caused us to be born again. The NIV® says He has given us new birth and the Greek says He begot us again. The meaning is clear that we are born again. Also, the more famous verse is John 3:3, *In reply Jesus declared, "I tell you the truth, no one can see the kingdom of God unless he is born again."* (NIV®) There is also James 1:18 *He chose to give us birth through the word of truth, that we might be a kind of firstfruits of all he created.* (NIV®) 1 Peter 1:23 *for you have been born again not of seed which is perishable but imperishable, that is, through the living and abiding word of God.* (NASB)

I am struck by the fact that three different authors of books in the Bible have mentioned this phenomenon that is the beginning of Christian life. It wasn't just John, but also Peter and James. Like Nicodemus, the person who asked me didn't understand. It was babbling to him. He claimed to be a Christian but his life didn't demonstrate it. There is no getting around the fact that something changes in people when they become Christians. If nothing changes, then there has not been a new birth. If I had continued in my ways after being born again I wouldn't be able to claim to be born again. By the way, I know I changed because the person who asked me the question wanted me to go back to my former habits, which had become disgusting to me.

In these last two verses, being born again is linked to the Word of God. It seems clear that without His Word, we can't become born again. 1 Peter 2:2 says that as newborn babies we should crave the pure milk of the Word. One of the things which happened after being born again is that I had a desire to read the Bible. Even more amazing was that I could understand it! A man at a men's breakfast group asked the others how we could understand the Bible. I don't remember the exact passage because it was many years ago, but it was evident that this person either was not born again or so infrequently in the Word that he had stagnated or never grown.

Hebrews 5:12-14 *You have been believers so long now that you ought to be teaching others. Instead, you need someone to teach you again the basic things about God's word. You are like babies who need milk and cannot eat solid food. For someone who lives on milk is still an infant and doesn't know how to do what is right. Solid food is for those who are mature, who through training have the skill to recognize the difference between right and wrong.* (NLT)

One reason for this book is that I don't want to be in the position of only knowing the basics and not being able to use the Word to tell the difference between good and evil. When I face situations, I want to be able, first of all, to recognize that something might be wrong with the picture. If my only view of life is what I get from the world (TV, magazines, movies, newspapers, Dr. Phil, teachers, professors, conservative or liberal talk show hosts, etc.) then I may easily stroll through life sinning blatantly and not have a clue that I'm dishonoring

God. However, I want my worldview to be shaped by God's Word so that I can see that something is wrong. The next thing is to formulate and carry out actions which are also shaped by God's Word. I can't do that if all I'm doing is reading the Bible briefly or sporadically. I need to dig into His Word so I don't just walk away after my time in the Word and not be moved closer to what God wants.

I may be born again, but I also need to keep on growing. I pray that is everyone's desire.

Living Hope – 1 Peter 1:3

Praise be to the God and Father of our Lord Jesus Christ! In his great mercy he has given us new birth into a living hope through the resurrection of Jesus Christ from the dead. (NIV®)

God the Father has given me a living hope through the resurrection of Jesus Christ. I need to ponder that for a moment. How many people think God is out to get us, to keep us under His thumb and make our lives miserable? But this verse says He gives me a living hope. A living hope as opposed to what, a dying hope? Yes, my hope is not just that I will eventually wind up in heaven where everything will be better, even though there is nothing wrong with that. Heaven is certainly something I should keep at the forefront of my mind.

I better digress and define hope. "A wish or desire accompanied by confident expectation of its fulfillment." This is not the "I hope it won't rain today" type of wishful thinking. This is confidence that I will get something that I have not yet received based on the authority and power of God who has promised it.

Romans 5:1-8 tells me what that hope is all about. I have peace with God.His goal isn't to make me miserable. When I face bad things, instead of blaming God, I know that the troubles are there to produce perseverance, character, and hope. I am confident of this because my confidence is in God who has promised it. How can I be so confident? Verse 5 says that hope doesn't disappoint me because God has poured out His love into my heart through the Holy Spirit, whom He has given me. It isn't me and my ability, but it is the Holy Spirit who gives me that confidence.

Romans 5:1-8 ties back to 1 Peter 1:3 as it explains that at just the right time, when I couldn't do anything to help myself, Jesus died for me – the ungodly person that I was. God demonstrates His love for me that while I was still his enemy and totally opposed to everything He is, while I was doing everything in my power to insult and hurt Him (even though I thought I was being a very nice guy), Jesus died for me.

Now with a God like that, how could I not have hope that helps me live each day?

Romans 8:23-25 *Not only so, but we ourselves, who have the firstfruits of the Spirit, groan inwardly as we wait eagerly for our adoption as sons, the redemption of our bodies. For in this hope we were saved. But hope that is seen is no hope at all. Who hopes for what he already has? But if we hope for what we do not yet have, we wait for it patiently.* (NIV®)

Ok, some of that hope is also knowing that this isn't all there is. This life will someday be over and when it is, I will be with Jesus. Again, there is confident expectation that it will occur. My body will be redeemed and I will no longer have to put up with the physical or spiritual weaknesses I now have. I have to wait patiently for that day to come. One thing about growing older is that I know that day is closer than it was yesterday.

1 John 3:2-3 *Beloved, we are God's children now; it does not yet appear what we shall be, but we know that when he appears we shall be like him, for we shall see him as he is. And every one who thus hopes in him purifies himself as he is pure.* (RSV)

So, because of this hope that I have, I don't sit around and do whatever I want. Instead, because I will someday be like Jesus, I need to purify myself now. If I'm not trying to become pure then I'm simply proving that Jesus isn't my Lord and that I really don't care what He wants.

Jesus had to die to give me this hope. His resurrection proves that His death wasn't meaningless but that He can give me the power by His Holy Spirit to live a godly life and purify myself.

Our Inheritance – 1 Peter 1:4

*… and into an inheritance that can never perish, spoil or fade —
kept in heaven for you …*(NIV®)

Not only am I given new birth into a living hope but I'm also
given an inheritance. The NAS version says to obtain this inheritance.
Unfortunately the word obtain is italicized which means it isn't in the
original Greek. Obtain clarifies the meaning since it doesn't seem like
I can be born into an inheritance. That is something I get or obtain
when another person dies. I don't usually think about the future
benefits of heaven as an inheritance but it fits because Jesus is the one
who died so I can go there when I die. That is another strange thought
– I have to die (unless Jesus comes back first) before I can receive the
inheritance.

In Hebrews 9:15-17 it says that Christ is the mediator of a new
covenant (from which comes the term New Testament) so that I may
receive the promised eternal inheritance because Jesus has died. The
Greek word for covenant and will (used in verse 16) is the same –
diatheke (dee-ath-ay'-kay). The verses go on to explain that for a will
to be in force, the death of the one who made it must be proven. Now
I want to go off with a big explanation of the proof of Jesus' death
and resurrection but then I'd never finish this thought. Besides, I did
that a long time ago. I've included in the appendix if you are
interested. The current benefit of the inheritance is found in Hebrews
10:16 *"This is the covenant I will make with them after that time, says
the Lord. I will put my laws in their hearts, and I will write them on
their minds."* (NIV®)

I need that law in my heart and mind, otherwise I'm without
hope. In the past, before I was born again, my only hope for heaven
was to be 100% obedient to all of God's laws. The problem with that
is that I can't be 100% obedient. I don't know anyone who can.
Neither does God know of anyone who can. So the law was put there
to show that I need someone to be a mediator for me. 1 John 2:1-2 *My
dear children, I am writing this to you so that you will not sin. But if
anyone does sin, we have an advocate who pleads our case before the
Father. He is Jesus Christ, the one who is truly righteous. He himself
is the sacrifice that atones for our sins—and not only our sins but the
sins of all the world.* (NLT) Now, of course, that doesn't give me the
right to blatantly sin but Jesus does defend me and has paid the
penalty for me. With His law in my heart and mind, I now have a

desire to obey. Before it was all external obedience but not from my heart.

Now I want to get back to the inheritance that is kept in heaven for me. The key thing in 1 Peter 1:4 is that it can never – and I need to emphasize the word never – be diminished in any way. It is kept for me by the power of the almighty God. He has promised it in these verses. Is there anything I can do that will remove that inheritance? No. Is there anything that anyone else can do to remove it? No. It is based on the one who has promised it.

Ephesians 1:13-14 *And you also were included in Christ when you heard the word of truth, the gospel of your salvation. Having believed, you were marked in him with a seal, the promised Holy Spirit, who is a deposit guaranteeing our inheritance until the redemption of those who are God's possession — to the praise of his glory.* (NIV®) The Holy Spirit who gives me hope is my guarantee that I will receive that inheritance. He will keep me until I die or Jesus returns.

That inheritance is like a divine 401(k). My inheritance is a mansion (John 14:2) and the right to reign with Christ (Revelation 3:21, 5:20, 20:6). That is the employer's input to my 401(k). My input is found in Matthew 6:19-21 (store up treasures in heaven). The great thing is that this is kept safe for me. No depressions, recession, moth, rust, thieves, or anything else will be able to diminish it.

Guaranteed Long Life – 1 Peter 1:5

Who are protected by the power of God through faith for a salvation ready to be revealed in the last time. (NASB)

OK, so I'm done with the inheritance but this next verse is really cool. I am protected by the power of God. I know that many people believe that they can lose their salvation if they turn away from God. I think this is one of the verses which support the fact that I will be kept safe until that salvation is completed. There seems to be a caveat in the verse as it states that the power of God is available by faith. Does that mean I have the ability to lose my faith and then I will no longer be protected and could lose my salvation? Well, if my faith was dependent on my own ability to remain faithful then I could certainly lose my salvation. However, my faith is not in myself, but it is in God and His ability to protect me.

A very familiar verse is Philippians 1:6 *being confident of this, that he who began a good work in you will carry it on to completion until the day of Christ Jesus.* (NIV®) I don't think God is someone who will not finish what He started. Unbelievers may argue that, but I believe the book of Revelation is God's plan for the end of this world and the beginning of a new world to come. I know the end of the story because I've read it. In the same way, I believe that He isn't going to dump me if I don't progress at a perfect rate or if I fall on the way. He will keep on working in me and won't give up.

Jude 24-25 *Now to him who is able to keep you from falling and to present you without blemish before the presence of his glory with rejoicing, to the only God, our Savior through Jesus Christ our Lord, be glory, majesty, dominion, and authority, before all time and now and for ever. Amen.* (RSV) This is one of my favorite memory verses because it affirms that when the end comes I will stand before my God without any blemishes. I know that I will stand there with great joy because He isn't going to bring up all my sins and ugly things I've done in my life. It will be to His glory and not mine because everyone who sees me standing there will know I don't deserve it. It is only because of Jesus and His sacrifice that I can stand there.

So I've looked at what others have said in Scripture about what they think God will do. Another set of my favorite verses is in John 10:27-30 *My sheep hear my voice, and I know them, and they follow me; and I give them eternal life, and they shall never perish, and no one shall snatch them out of my hand. My Father, who has given them to me, is greater than all, and no one is able to snatch them out of the Father's hand. I and the Father are one."* (RSV) These are Jesus' own words. First Jesus says He has given me eternal life and that life is so firm and solid in His mind that He can say I will never perish. Wow! His promise is something I can hold on to and it is apparent that He is holding me in His hand. So the question is whether or not someone can pull me out of His hand.

I must diverge. I remember seeing the Kung Fu TV series where Grasshopper finally is able to snatch a pebble from his master's hand and then it was time to leave. My Master isn't some aging martial arts expert. My Master is eternal, all-powerful, and all knowing. If someone were to try to snatch me out of God's hand, He would know it way before hand. He would be able to prevent it even if He didn't know it. He is eternal so He doesn't get weak or senile so He can't hold on to me.

Some have argued with me and said they could chose to reject God and therefore lose their salvation. My answer is that since I'm saved and in His hand I don't want to leave. If I did want to leave then I wasn't really in His hand to start with – I didn't really believe and have faith. Even if it crossed my mind to do something like that (and that happens), He protects me. Otherwise, I would be able to say that I'm greater than God and am able to snatch myself out of His hand.

I also like these verses in John because Jesus reiterates that He is God by claiming to be one with God. "Ah!" you say, "He didn't claim to be God but only one in purpose with God." When I look at John 10:31-33, I see that the Jews who were listening to Him clearly understood that Jesus claimed to be God and said they would stone Him for making the claim. In the verses following (John 10:34-39) Jesus didn't deny the charge.

So Jesus is the one in whom I have faith and He gives me eternal life and guarantees that it will always be that way.

Sanctification – 1 Peter 1:5

Who are protected by the power of God through faith for a salvation ready to be revealed in the last time. (NASB)
I normally think of salvation as something that happened to me when I turned to Jesus and was born again as stated above. The ending of this verse refers to a salvation that is different. My understanding is that there are three stages of salvation. John 5:24 *Verily, verily, I say unto you, He that heareth my word, and believeth on him that sent me, hath everlasting life, and shall not come into condemnation; but is passed from death unto life.* (KJV) This is the initial start of my salvation. There was a point in my life some 35 years ago when I heard Jesus' words, understood them for the first time, and believed. At that point I crossed over (NIV®) from death into life – eternal life. At that point, I knew I was no longer condemned.

The second part of salvation is my daily growth in Christ. Some people call this a process of sanctification. This process is described in part in Philippians 3:7-14 where Paul says that he considers everything that he had gained in the world (prestige, power, and whatever) nothing in comparison to knowing Jesus. In fact, he had to give it all up when he became a Christian. I didn't have to give up as much as some people do in other parts of the world. Would I give it up, if I had to? I certainly hope I wouldn't even have to think about it. He describes the process of sanctification as not having his own righteousness but the righteousness that comes from faith (initial start of salvation). He goes on to say he wants to know the power of Jesus' resurrection, share in Jesus' sufferings, and become more like Jesus.

In Ephesians 1:19-23 Paul describes the power of Jesus' resurrection. He says that power is for me because I believe. That is the power to live a holy life. Learning to rely on His power is what brings me closer to being like Jesus. Back in Philippians, Paul also goes on to admit he hasn't become the perfect Christian but he puts the past behind him to push on to that goal. I need to remember that when I sin (I'm getting tired of people saying they made wrong choices, messed up, or made a mistake – I just about typed one of those instead of saying sin), I need to repent, put it behind me and get back on the path to becoming more like Jesus. With Paul, I admit that I'm nowhere near that goal, but I have experienced His power to overcome sin.

1 John 3:1-3 says that God has lavished His love on me so that I'm a child of His. I will be like Jesus and I don't know exactly what that will be like. Because I will and I have that hope, I purify myself because Jesus is pure. It doesn't mean I sit around and wait for Jesus to wave a magic wand and I become pure. It means I have to work with Him, to yield to Him so that it will happen.

Finally, the last stage of salvation is when I'm safely in heaven. That is the reference in 1 Peter 1:5. It is in the last time. When Jesus comes back, sets all things straight on the earth, rules for 1,000 years to give mankind a last chance at salvation, then starts over with a new heaven and a new earth (Revelation 20 and 21). I wasn't made for life on this earth; I was made for eternal life. Through sin, that life was forfeit. Through Jesus, that life is redeemed. Everyone was made for eternal life, but unfortunately, not everyone will make it and that, too, is described in Revelation 20 and 21.

So I'm eagerly waiting for the culmination of my salvation when Jesus is revealed to all.

Rejoicing in Trials – 1 Peter 1:6-7

In this you greatly rejoice, though now for a little while you may have had to suffer grief in all kinds of trials. These have come so that your faith — of greater worth than gold, which perishes even though refined by fire — may be proved genuine and may result in praise, glory and honor when Jesus Christ is revealed. (NIV®)

Just before I sat down to write about these verses and what they mean to me, I read an e-mail from Pakistan that included a news article. Apparently the Taliban around the city of Sargodha sent a letter to several Christian pastors and Christian schools in the city. The letter said that Christians should convert to Islam, pay an Islamic tax imposed on religious minorities, known as 'Jizya tax', or leave the country. If Christians refuse to accept these choices, Christians "will be killed, their property and homes will be burnt to ashes and their women treated as sex slaves," said the letter. The Christians "themselves would be responsible for this," the letter added.

If I were in Sargodha, would I be rejoicing that my faith was being tested? What would I do? Would I remain and take my chances that the government would protect my family and me? Would I take everything I could carry and flee? It is hard for me to understand what I would do; however, I have made up my mind that I would rejoice.

I've been through some personal trials in my past; family, health and other things, but nothing that threatened my life. I have felt God's presence in those trials. I know He will sustain me in trials. I have resolved that I will listen for God's direction if this were to happen to me. He may lead me to flee as many of the early Christian did when persecution broke out against the Church in Jerusalem (Acts 8). Most fled to other parts of Israel and even beyond. The amazing thing is that when this occurred, the Word of God spread faster than it would have in a time of peace. Perhaps I would flee and thereby take the Gospel to some area where the people needed to hear it.

If I had to stay in place and was threatened to renounce Christ or die, my verse would be: Mark 8:36-37 *"For what does it profit a man to gain the whole world, and forfeit his soul?"* (NASB) At this time in my life, I have made up my mind that I would not renounce Jesus for any reason. If it cost me my life then I would be in a better place.

Why do I say this so confidently? It's because I know that if I don't make the choice now, when not threatened, I will have a harder time when faced with it later. This same principle applies to most critical decisions. If I am faced with an easy way to cheat and get away with it (on my job, taxes, wife, you name it), then what makes me think I will not cheat if I haven't already made up my mind to be honest even when no one is watching?

Matthew 5:9-12 *"Blessed are the peacemakers, for they shall be called sons of God. Blessed are those who are persecuted for righteousness' sake, for theirs is the kingdom of heaven. Blessed are you when men revile you and persecute you and utter all kinds of evil against you falsely on my account. Rejoice and be glad, for your reward is great in heaven, for so men persecuted the prophets who were before you."* (RSV)

Jesus' words are hard to swallow sometimes. In the U.S. there are many churches that teach a Christian should be healthy and wealthy or they are living in a state of unfaithfulness. I can't help to wonder why they ignore the clear teaching of Jesus that some will be persecuted. There are many other verses which also state this is the norm for Christians. Peter opened his letter to those who had already been scattered to other countries because of persecution. I certainly don't think that I should be exempt just because I live in the 21st century.

Jesus' words bring out the truth that I'm not living for this world. My reward will be in heaven. If I fix my eyes on this world and its rewards, then my decisions and goals will be oriented toward the temporary things of this world. When I eventually die, then all those temporary things will be gone and the eternal things that I should have worked for will not have been achieved (2 Corinthians 4:16-18).

For my brothers and sisters in Pakistan, I pray daily for you. I pray that you would remain strong in your faith and not surrender. I pray that you would have wisdom to flee or stay. I pray that plans to aid you in some way will occur. I pray that you will not show fear for that is Satan's tool to keep others from becoming Christians. I pray that you will be able to rejoice in all circumstances (1 Thessalonians 5:16). And I pray for peace for you.

Seeing is Believing – Not! 1 Peter 1:8-9

Without having seen him you love him; though you do not now see him you believe in him and rejoice with unutterable and exalted joy. As the outcome of your faith you obtain the salvation of your souls. (RSV)

I think one of the hardest parts of believing in Jesus is the fact He isn't a visible person. As I studied English literature in college, I took a class on fairy tales as literature. The class described how fairy tales change over time. I've seen the same things in those urban legends that are passed around on the internet. Someone gets an e-mail and tweaks it a little bit to make it sound a little more realistic for his friends or his neighborhood. A name or a place is changed; most certainly the date so that it appears urgent. This is what I once believed about the Bible and Jesus. I thought that from the time of Jesus, people kept tweaking the Gospels to fit the needs of the time or to make them more acceptable. I believed that Jesus' appearances after His death were some of the things that were tweaked.

After a thorough study of early manuscripts and other document, of which thousands have been preserved, literary scholars agree that the Bible has not gone through the changes that occur with folk and fairy tales. With that in mind, these two verses celebrate a key in the Christian faith. Even though I have not seen Jesus, I believe in Him, but more importantly, I love Him. I believe because of what has been written. It isn't a faith based on fantasy or speculation. A careful examination of the Gospels and current medical knowledge absolutely confirm that there is no way Jesus could have survived His crucifixion as some skeptics have claimed. Yet He is alive!

The book of Acts was written by a physician and researcher – Luke's accounts are very trustworthy because of his scholarly approach and other historical facts in his writing can be verified. Acts 1:3 *After his suffering, he showed himself to these men and gave many convincing proofs that he was alive. He appeared to them over a period of forty days and spoke about the kingdom of God.* (NIV®) I am struck by the fact that Luke says Jesus gave many convincing proofs that He was alive. 1 Corinthians 15:5-7 says that Jesus appeared to over 500 people. Some of these people were alive when Paul wrote this. The silence of the rest of literature opposing these statements is another proof that Jesus is alive.

With all this proof, I still have to have faith. John 20:29 *Jesus said to him, "Because you have seen Me, have you believed? Blessed are they who did not see, and yet believed."* (NASB) I consider myself blessed because I haven't seen Jesus and have believed. There is something inexpressible about knowing that I believe and didn't require Jesus to appear before me to make me believe. Paul's experience on the way to Damascus may have been life changing and very dramatic, but he missed the joy of believing without seeing. I'm trying to get words around this but I'm not doing a very good job. That's probably because Peter was right. In the RSV it is unutterable; in the NIV® and others it is inexpressible; in the KJV it is unspeakable. That joy is described as glorious. Just thinking about it gives me a sense of the presence of God from Whom all glory comes. It is inexpressible.

The outcome of this faith is the salvation of my soul. For this I am very thankful. I can think back on the time before I believed and can see that I was lost.

Prophesied Salvation – 1 Peter 1:10-12

The prophets who prophesied of the grace that was to be yours searched and inquired about this salvation; they inquired what person or time was indicated by the Spirit of Christ within them when predicting the sufferings of Christ and the subsequent glory. It was revealed to them that they were serving not themselves but you, in the things which have now been announced to you by those who preached the good news to you through the Holy Spirit sent from heaven, things into which angels long to look. (RSV)

I've always wondered if the prophets and writers of the O.T. knew that what they were writing was a prophecy for the near future or something way beyond. Several of the Psalms have statements in them that are astounding. To appreciate it fully, I imagined that I'm David as I'm writing Psalm 16. As I write praises and thanksgiving to God, suddenly these next two verses come to my mind and I write them down. Psalm 16:9-10 *Therefore my heart is glad and my tongue rejoices; my body also will rest secure, because you will not abandon me to the grave, nor will you let your Holy One see decay.* (NIV®) Whoa! Where did that come from? (Of course, Holy One is capitalized so that I can recognize that it is a reference to the coming Messiah, but David didn't have that advantage.) As David, I have to stop and ask God, "Are you saying that I won't decay after I'm in the grave? What does that mean? Will you resurrect me?" Now, did God answer David and tell him that he was writing about the coming Messiah or did he just keep on writing? Did He even comprehend that a Messiah was on the way or did that understanding come later? According to Peter, David did stop writing and started asking God a lot of questions. I certainly would.

Perhaps, as David, I would think back to Job 19:25-27 *I know that my Redeemer lives, and that in the end he will stand upon the earth. And after my skin has been destroyed, yet in my flesh I will see God; I myself will see him with my own eyes — I, and not another. How my heart yearns within me!* (NIV®) I would sit back and understand that my Redeemer will have to suffer death but will be raised from the dead before He rots in the grave. I, however, will die and my body will decompose but somehow, I too, will be resurrected with a new body that will be able to see my Savior. Yes, my heart also yearns within me to see that day. It is all part of the hope that Peter has just mentioned.

Another great verse is Psalm 110:1 *The Lord says to my Lord: "Sit at my right hand until I make your enemies a footstool for your feet."* (NIV®) David must have certainly wondered about the beginning of this verse. Jesus used this verse to clarify unequivocally that the Messiah had to be a descendant of David as well as God because David called Him "Lord." My salvation is in Jesus because He is the only one who can satisfy the requirements of divinity as well as an earthly lineage of David.

My salvation is in one who can pay for my sins. Psalm 49:7-9 *No man can redeem the life of another or give to God a ransom for him — the ransom for a life is costly, no payment is ever enough — that he should live on forever and not see decay.* (NIV®) Peter already talked about the security of our inheritance. When a son of Korah penned this Psalm, he was declaring that salvation can't come from a mere man. Did he wonder how we could ever have eternal life if there was no way anyone could pay for it? Did he understand that Jesus, being God in the flesh, would be the only ransom, the only payment that would be able to give him eternal life? I'll bet he looked at that verse and shook his head and kept on writing because he knew that someone in the future would see it and understand.

When Peter talks about the predictions of the suffering Christ, two passages come to mind. The first is Isaiah 53. Isaiah details Jesus' suffering and the reason for it. My sins caused Him to be pierced. He took the punishment of my sins. He was assigned a grave with the wicked (the two thieves crucified at the same time), yet buried in a rich man's tomb. All this, even though He did nothing wrong. It was God's will to do this to Him. He bore all our sins, not just mine. I have a hard time imagining what was going through Isaiah's mind as he wrote this. Perhaps the Holy Spirit let him know that a future generation would need to know this to explain Jesus' purpose during His first visit to the earth.

The second passage is Psalm 22. The details of the crucifixion were recorded here a thousand years before that horrible death was invented. His hands and feet were pierced. He could count His bones after the flogging. Even the detail that they cast lots for His clothing was written down. How could David not wonder about what he was writing? It certainly didn't happen to him. Yet, the Holy Spirit must have let him know that this was a future event that had something to do with salvation, otherwise he would have pushed the delete key and started over again.

This salvation that Jesus has purchased for me and everyone else is just too astounding to comprehend. Hundreds of years before Jesus, people were writing about it. It is so astounding that angels even wonder about it.

Be Prepared – 1 Peter 1:13-16

Therefore, prepare your minds for action; be self-controlled; set your hope fully on the grace to be given you when Jesus Christ is revealed. As obedient children, do not conform to the evil desires you had when you lived in ignorance. But just as he who called you is holy, so be holy in all you do; for it is written: "Be holy, because I am holy." (NIV®)

I re-read the passages that precede this since Peter started it off with "therefore." He really packed a lot of theology into those first twelve verses. Most of it relates to salvation, how God has brought it about, and what we can expect in the world. Therefore – my response is to be mentally prepared and to be holy.

When I wrote about persecutions, I emphasized that what I have decided ahead of time helps me to be prepared to react in a godly manner when life presents difficult choices. Peter affirms that this is exactly what I need to do. Because of all he has written I am to prepare my mind for action. An example of this is found in Job 31:1 *"I made a covenant with my eyes not to look with lust at a young woman."* (NLT) Job knew that if he didn't make up his mind to control his thoughts when he saw a beautiful young woman, he would be in trouble. The verse suggests he did this by averting his eyes so that he would not be tempted.

I remember going to a conference about family behavior. The speaker went to this verse in Job and explained how children watch their parents. When Dad takes that long or second look at a woman as she walks past, both sons and daughters notice. The daughter sees how the scantily clad woman pleases her dad and consciously or subconsciously decides to dress that way when she is allowed. The son watches and sees that this is the way men behave and emulates his dad's behavior possibly leading into a life immersed in pornography and lust. With only his eyes Dad has led his children into behavior that can easily leads them into sexual sin. How does Mom react? She feels betrayed and certainly not the only woman in her husband's life. She may also compromise her moral standards to try to please her husband.

I watch old re-runs of the TV show "Emergency!" In nearly every episode, and more than once in most, firefighter Johnny turns half way around and gives a nurse the "look over." I'm sure that the message is clear that this is natural and normal behavior for a single man. But it isn't what Peter is telling me. Peter is telling me to be self-controlled. I can't be self-controlled until I have prepared my mind. I need to know where the battle is and take my thoughts captive to make them obedient to Christ (2 Corinthians 10:5), not to Hollywood, not even to conservative talk show host. The way I look at a woman is a good example of the way I should order my life and be prepared to combat sinful desires.

My motivation is the grace to be given to me when Jesus is revealed. When I stand before Jesus, He will present me without fault and with great joy before His Father. He has cleansed me and

forgiven me but I don't want to be presumptuous about that and think
that I can do whatever I want.

Out of gratitude to that wonderful salvation, I want to obey Jesus.
Peter encourages this obedience to Jesus. He tells me that I should not
be living my life the way I did before I came to Christ. Back then, I
was ignorant about what was right and wrong. I shouldn't be now.
Hebrews 5:14 *But solid food is for the mature, for those who have
their faculties trained by practice to distinguish good from evil.*
(RSV) If I want to know right from wrong, I need to understand it
from God's Word and put it into practice. I need to leave those old
habits behind and form new, godly habits based on the sure Word of
God.

The final reason for being prepared and leaving the old, sinful
habits behind is that God is holy. He wants me to be holy just as He
is. Will that happen today? No. Does that give me an excuse for not
working on it? No. Ultimately, I want to be holy because my Father is
holy. I want to be like Him.

Fear God? – 1 Peter 1:17

*Since you call on a Father who judges each man's work
impartially, live your lives as strangers here in reverent fear.* (NIV®)

I call God my Father. That should be quite a sobering thought and
action. A good son should emulate his father. There is a phrase that I
haven't heard for a long time, "He is a chip off the old block." The
reference is to a child who looks and acts like his dad. It used to be a
matter of honor for a son to follow in the footsteps of his father. I
wonder if names like Wilson, Johnson, and others were carried on
because the son acted and behaved in such a way that people could
tell his father was Will or John. Since I have been adopted into a new
family (Ephesians 1:5; 3:14,15), I want bring honor to my new family
by my actions. My new family name is Christian – which means little
Christ.

Many of the Jews who challenged Jesus claimed to have God as
their Father (John 8:41). They first claimed Abraham as their father in
verse 39, but Jesus challenged them to act like Abraham and not try to
kill Him. They then appealed to God as their Father. Jesus responded
by saying that if they had God as their Father then they would love

Jesus. Jesus even went so far as to say that they had the devil as their father in verses 42-44. Jesus' argument concludes with John 8:47 *"He who belongs to God hears what God says. The reason you do not hear is that you do not belong to God."* (NIV®)

I have to take a little side trip here to say I've met people who claim to love God but don't want to have anything to do with Jesus. Based on Jesus' conversation with His detractors, I have some bad news for anyone who thinks of Jesus as less than God in the flesh and don't recognize Him as the only way to God the Father. You are on the wrong path and it isn't leading to heaven (John 14:6).

I think this is where the reverent fear comes in. I know that God isn't going to judge me on the curve. He isn't going to weigh my life on some kind of scale that balances out the good and bad to see if I'm worthy of heaven. He is going to look at me and if He finds even one thing that's wrong, I'm under a sentence of death. That is absolutely scary. Have I been listening to what God says? Do I call Him Father but am I like the Pharisees who sought to justify themselves by their observance of man-made traditions? If so, then I should have a deathly fear of God.

Of course, as I've already discussed, it isn't by my good works that I'm saved and Peter will go into that even more in the next few verses. I just want to get a good grasp on the fact that without Jesus' sacrifice, I should be deathly afraid of God and His judgment. However, in light of the fact that I am saved, that horrible fear changes to a reverent fear. What's the difference? It is the knowledge that without Jesus and His forgiveness, my Father in heaven would not spare me. However, I also know the love God has for me. Romans 5:8 *But God demonstrates His own love toward us, in that while we were yet sinners, Christ died for us.* (NASB)

Sometimes, I forget about the awesomeness of God and I'm caught up in the brotherhood of Jesus and being in the family of Christ so that the Father becomes a bit to "familiar." I should still hold Him in great respect. Yes, I can come before the throne of grace with confidence (Hebrews 4:16), but that confidence shouldn't cause me to come with a disrespectful attitude. I want to achieve a balance between the tender mercies of my Father who will someday wipe away every tear (Revelation 7:17, 21:4), and the knowledge that without Jesus I would be horribly lost.

I want my life to bring honor to my Father, and that means I need to have the proper respect for Him.

Ransomed – 1 Peter 1:18-21

You know that you were ransomed from the futile ways inherited from your fathers, not with perishable things such as silver or gold, but with the precious blood of Christ, like that of a lamb without blemish or spot. (RSV) *20 He was chosen before the creation of the world, but was revealed in these last times for your sake.* (NIV®) *21 Through him you have confidence in God, who raised him from the dead and gave him glory, so that your faith and hope are in God.* (RSV)

I've been ransomed. It strikes me that most governments, while trying to free kidnapped people, are opposed to paying a ransom for their release. All of mankind was kidnapped by Satan when he tempted Adam and Eve in the garden and got them to rebel against God. Ever since then, children born to their descendants have been born into slavery to sin. The futile ways I've inherited is my nature to sin. I was no different until Jesus ransomed me. A ransom is the price demanded by the kidnapper or slave owner for the freedom of the captive. Usually the kidnapper establishes the price, but in this case, God established the price for my freedom.

The price for freedom from sin and adoption into the family of God had to be something a whole lot more than the things of this world. No amount of money could buy my freedom. Money is worthless in eternity. Previously I quoted Psalm 49:7-9 which expressed God's position on the ransom for a life. God says no payment is ever enough. No wonder Peter says the blood of Jesus is precious. In human terms, it is more precious than any amount of earthly riches. Why blood? Because Leviticus 17:11 says that life is in the blood and Hebrews 9:22 explains that without the shedding of blood there can be no forgiveness.

I think about all Jesus had to do to provide that for us. John 1:1-3 establishes that Jesus is God, is eternal, and created all things. He had to give all that up in order to take on a body that could bleed and die. If He hadn't done that but came as some super human being, He couldn't die. There isn't anything (like kryptonite which weakens

Superman) that could have made Jesus vulnerable. He had to give up His God nature on His own. Once it was established that He could die, He volunteered to go to the cross to pay the price for our sins and rebellion. That's what Philippians 2:6-8 is talking about.

Peter points out that Jesus was chosen before the creation of time to do this. The timing is confirmed in Ephesians 1:4, Titus 1:2, and Revelation 13:8. I am astounded to think that before I or even the earth existed, God decided He would come to the earth to redeem fallen mankind and me by dying on a cross. He made that choice even before He created Adam and Eve. Jesus is not a martyr in the sense that He had no control over the situation. He is a martyr because he was a willing volunteer to take the punishment and pay the price that we couldn't.

The result is that I have confidence in God through Jesus. When I believe in Jesus, I believe in God. God's plan included raising Jesus from the dead. His plan for me was not to let me wallow in my sin but he has restored me from that state and given me a position in His family. I'm redeemed!

Love One Another – 1 Peter 1:22-25

Now that you have purified yourselves by obeying the truth so that you have sincere love for your brothers, love one another deeply, from the heart. For you have been born again, not of perishable seed, but of imperishable, through the living and enduring word of God. For, "All men are like grass, and all their glory is like the flowers of the field; the grass withers and the flowers fall, but the word of the Lord stands forever." And this is the word that was preached to you. (NIV®)

It is a given that I have purified myself by obeying the truth. Oh, I have to stop and think about that one for a while. Have I really purified myself by obeying the truth? I don't think I can stand up to perfect scrutiny of my life, my thoughts, or my habits. Yes, I believe Jesus has purified me, but there is still an ongoing process of becoming more like Jesus. I've a long way to go.

One proof I haven't made it is that comment in the verses about having sincere love for my brothers. NASB says that I should now have fervent love for others. Fervent? Synonyms for fervent are: keen, avid, ardent, enthusiastic, passionate, zealous, and fanatical. Well, that just isn't me. What a lame excuse! I've heard it from others and now I'm using it myself. That's what the power of the Holy Spirit is all about, changing me from who I am into what God wants me to be. Ok, Lord, I need a lot of help in this area.

The whole reason for loving each other is wrapped up in being born again through the Word of God. The Word of God can change me into that loving person. Peter quoted from Isaiah 40:6-8 to contrast the brevity of man to the eternal nature of the Word of God. Jesus stated in Matthew 5:18 *"For truly, I say to you, till heaven and earth pass away, not an iota, not a dot, will pass from the law until all is accomplished."* (RSV) Since Jesus is God and He is also called the Word in John 1:1, I am pretty confident that the Word is going to be around forever.

Since my life is so brief on earth it only makes sense to love one another. All the other stuff of the world is passing away. It is temporary but my brothers and sisters in Christ are not. We will all be together in eternity. How embarrassing it will be for me to meet a fellow believer in heaven and realize that there was no love for that person on earth. Ouch!

How can I show love to others? A good verse is 1 John 3:16-18 *We know love by this, that He laid down His life for us; and we ought to lay down our lives for the brethren. But whoever has the world's goods, and beholds his brother in need and closes his heart against him, how does the love of God abide in him? Little children, let us not love with word or with tongue, but in deed and truth.* (NASB) I am overwhelmed sometimes at the abundance I have here in the West and the poverty of my brethren in other parts of the world. I'm helping poor Christians in a Pakistan city with Bibles, school supplies, and other aid. If anyone wants to help, you can visit my web site at http://pakistan.rayruppert.com/.

First Peter – Chapter Two

The Basics – 1 Peter 2:1-3

Therefore, rid yourselves of all malice and all deceit, hypocrisy, envy, and slander of every kind. Like newborn babies, crave pure spiritual milk, so that by it you may grow up in your salvation, now that you have tasted that the Lord is good. (NIV®)

In view of the previous verses about how temporary life is and that God's Word endures forever, I should rid myself of all these evils. Malice can also be translated as wickedness – that really encompasses a lot. Perhaps, if I had a grudge against someone or was engaged in witchcraft this might be more meaningful to me. For now, I don't relate.

Deceit seems to be lying or tricking someone to get something I wouldn't otherwise be able to have if I didn't resort to it. Hmm, truth in advertising… When I had online stores, this was something I needed to be careful about. I didn't want to deceive anyone about the products I sold or who I am or anything else. It is too easy to slip into this. Another thought in business is how to handle deductions for the business. I don't want to fudge so I can classify things as business expenses when they aren't. A tax consultant said I could write off my vacations if I took my laptop along and conducted my online business while on vacation. Come on now! I'm going to take hotel and family meals as business expenses just because I take time on the vacation to make sure stuff is running correctly? It may be permissible but I wouldn't have had those expenses if I were not on vacation. Sounds deceitful to me.

Hypocrisy is being two-faced; professing beliefs, feelings, or virtues that I don't hold. If I were to tell you how humble I am, that would be hypocrisy. If I told you I loved you and didn't or that I believed in Jesus but didn't, both would be hypocrisy. Jesus had a way of cutting to the heart of the matter in the religious realm of hypocrisy. Giving was a big thing. When the Pharisees blew trumpets to announce how much they were giving, not to honor God, but to get attentions for themselves, Jesus nailed them. When they kept their own rules and overrode God's commands, Jesus got them on that because it was for their own glorification, not God's. I can easily slip into writing this book, not for my original purpose to dig into the Word, but to get people who read it to look up to me. Same with any ministry, I slowly stop doing it for the right reasons and for my own pride.

Envy is another matter. It's too easy to envy what others have. How much of why I'm working is to have the things others have and how much is to use it for God's glory? It is just too easy to slip over the line. It's good for me to stop and think about this regularly.

I don't want to slander or bad mouth people either. It isn't my habit, but I know it is easy to judge and put someone down while sharing prayer needs or just talking about a "situation" with others who know about it. Lord, help me keep from doing that, too.

If I'm not in the Word of God, accepting it like a newborn baby, I can easily fall into all these things or never get out of them. Matthew 18:3 *"Truly, I say to you, unless you turn and become like children, you will never enter the kingdom of heaven."* (RSV) Until now, I hadn't drawn the connection between pure spiritual milk and what Jesus told his disciples. To be a kingdom citizen, I need to accept His Word and even crave it just like a child. How else can I avoid or get rid of these things? 1 Corinthians 14:20 says that I should be mature in my thinking. It starts with correct thinking (Philippians 4:8, 9), which transforms me by renewing my mind (Romans 12:2). The result is growth and maturity.

Peter's command to crave pure spiritual milk is a starting place. Hebrews 5:11-14 *About this we have much to say which is hard to explain, since you have become dull of hearing. For though by this time you ought to be teachers, you need some one to teach you again the first principles of God's word. You need milk, not solid food; for every one who lives on milk is unskilled in the word of righteousness, for he is a child. But solid food is for the mature, for those who have their faculties trained by practice to distinguish good from evil.* (RSV) I need to keep on in the Word and not just going over the basics. I need to start there and keep them but I need to push on also. A key in this verse is, "trained by practice to distinguish good from evil." Without training and practice, I'll remain a baby and not be able to determine if that tax deduction is really right regardless of what the tax consultant or tax code says.

I can grow up in my salvation this way. Getting rid of the bad stuff by learning to determine what is good and bad by the Word of God.

Ray Ruppert

Spiritual House – 1 Peter 2:4-8

Come to him, to that living stone, rejected by men but in God's sight chosen and precious; and like living stones be yourselves built into a spiritual house, to be a holy priesthood, to offer spiritual sacrifices acceptable to God through Jesus Christ. For it stands in scripture: "Behold, I am laying in Zion a stone, a cornerstone chosen and precious, and he who believes in him will not be put to shame." To you therefore who believe, he is precious, but for those who do not believe, "The very stone which the builders rejected has become the head of the corner," and "A stone that will make men stumble, a rock that will make them fall"; for they stumble because they disobey the word, as they were destined to do. (RSV)

Jesus is chosen and precious in God's sight yet rejected by men. I wonder how many other things are precious to God that I have rejected. How many precious gifts have I received in my life and have scorned them or thought they were a burden? Maybe I simply haven't been grateful for some of the things He has given. 1 Thessalonians 5:16-18 says that it is God's will for me to be joyful, pray continually and to give thanks in all circumstances. Jesus was rejected by mankind yet Hebrews 12:2 says that He considered it joy to go to the cross for me. When difficulties come, shouldn't I be joyful and thankful that I'm being molded and shaped by a loving Father who knows what's best for me?

That molding and shaping is to prepare me to be a spiritual house and a royal priesthood. People often call the church building the house of God. Does God live in houses built by man? Yes, He is everywhere but He dwells in us. Ephesians 2:22 *And in him you too are being built together to become a dwelling in which God lives by his Spirit.* (NIV®) It doesn't matter which denomination I belong to, I am part of the Church with a capital "C" because it is the body of Christ. However, that denomination had better be following Jesus or it will be like the church in Revelation 3:16b *I am about to spit you out of my mouth.* (NIV®)

So what is that spiritual sacrifice I can now offer as a royal priesthood? First I need to offer myself. That would be described in Romans 12:1 which says I should be offering my body as living

36

sacrifice to God. That pleases Him. I have a feeling many people who claim to be Christians haven't really understood that becoming a Christian requires a total surrender to God; it is a transfer of ownership. It isn't easy to do. I often forget and do my own thing.

Another sacrifice is praise. Hebrews 13:15 *Through him then let us continually offer up a sacrifice of praise to God, that is, the fruit of lips that acknowledge his name.* (RSV) In many parts of the world, this is more of a sacrifice than in other places. Acknowledging His name can also bring a death sentence. I certainly should be able to do that here where there is little threat. I need to do it more openly.

I think this leads directly into the cornerstone comments. If I'm afraid to acknowledge Jesus as my Lord then I will trip over Him. Jesus said in Matthew 12:30 that if I'm not with Him, I'm against Him. In Mark 8:38 He said that if I'm ashamed of Him now, then He will be ashamed of me when He comes back. That doesn't sound good. On the other hand, if I trust in Him now, I have confidence that I will be with Him when He comes back.

Then there is that last little bit of verse 8. Some stumble because that is their destiny. I can only say that I know Jesus. It is not my destiny to stumble. I had stumbled for a long time but not now. If you feel you are destined to stumble then you should know Jesus forgives and accepts right up to the last moment of life on earth. Just look at the thief on the cross. It was a last minute salvation for him. However, in the other Gospel accounts he had been cursing Jesus just as the other thief had. Yet he turned at the last minute to ask Jesus to remember him. The thieves knew their time was almost up. Few people know how imminent death is. The only way to know for sure whether you are destined to stumble or to be saved is to ask Jesus right now to be with you and surrender your life to Him. Otherwise, you may miss the opportunity and discover in eternity that you were destined to stumble but had many chances to change that destiny.

Chosen – 1 Peter 2:9-10

But you are a chosen people, a royal priesthood, a holy nation, a people belonging to God, that you may declare the praises of him who called you out of darkness into his wonderful light. Once you were not a people, but now you are the people of God; once you had not received mercy, but now you have received mercy. (NIV®)

I love these two verses. It is a great summary of the Gospel, where I was, and my new purpose. God has chosen me, along with all other Christians. That thought can be overwhelming.

When a new president takes office, he chooses his cabinet to serve him and help administer his office according to his policies. Many appointments are people who have shown their support prior to the election. A few are appointed for other political reason.

In some ways, it is the same with God. I didn't apply for the position of royal priest. I had no idea there was even such a position. But God chose me. Another similarity is that the position of royal priesthood is an appointment to administer God's policies. A priest is a mediator between God and man. Wait a minute, when Jesus died and the veil was torn, didn't the requirement for a priest end? Yes it did, for those who know Jesus. However, billions don't know Him and they need a priest. Paul explained it very clearly.

2 Corinthians 5:18-21 *All this is from God, who through Christ reconciled us to himself and gave us the ministry of reconciliation; that is, in Christ God was reconciling the world to himself, not counting their trespasses against them, and entrusting to us the message of reconciliation. So we are ambassadors for Christ, God making his appeal through us. We beseech you on behalf of Christ, be reconciled to God. For our sake he made him to be sin who knew no sin, so that in him we might become the righteousness of God.* (RSV)

God has already taken the first step. He has brought me back to himself in a friendly relationship. He has resolved the dispute between us. That restored relationship is available to everyone who is an enemy of God. However, most people don't realize there is a dispute. Some realize it and just don't know how to resolve it. They think they have to earn that relationship by their good behavior, rituals, etc. Since God has already made the way, He has called everyone who knows Him to be His ambassadors (or priests) to tell the rest of the world the way to God is open. The way is through Jesus.

As a priest, I come to God with offerings. Those offerings are the people whom I have told about Jesus. As the priest of the O.T. had to prepare the offerings, I have to prepare people to become a living sacrifice. I have to tell them that even though the price has been paid, there are still requirements like repentance and surrender to God.

Jesus paved the way to God by taking everyone's sins on Himself so that they can have the righteousness of God. To receive that gift of righteousness, they must surrender to Him. He is the conquering King and reconciliation is based on His rules, not man's. The ambassador or priest clearly describes the policies of the administration: freedom from sin if you are willing to be a slave to God.

Yeah, that's right, a slave to God. The job of the royal priest is a slave's job. The position of being God's people is slavery. The reward of being called out of darkness into God's marvelous light is a slave's reward. Receiving mercy is a benefit of being a slave as opposed to being an enemy. Romans 6:22 *But now that you have been set free from sin and have become slaves to God, the benefit you reap leads to holiness, and the result is eternal life.* (NIV®) Don't underestimate the benefits of holiness – the peace that comes with it, as well as eternal life – eternal pleasures at His right hand (Psalm 16:11).

The Flesh – 1 Peter 2:11-12

Beloved, I beseech you as aliens and exiles to abstain from the passions of the flesh that wage war against your soul. Maintain good conduct among the Gentiles, so that in case they speak against you as wrongdoers, they may see your good deeds and glorify God on the day of visitation. (RSV)

This is Peter talking to people who have been scattered to other nations because of persecution. How does this pertain to me? As mentioned before, I am an alien in this world and for that reason I should resist the passions of the flesh even more. When it comes to these passions, the Bible is quite clear about them.

Romans 13:13 *Let us behave properly as in the day, not in carousing and drunkenness, not in sexual promiscuity and sensuality, not in strife and jealousy.* Galatians 5:17-21 *For the flesh sets its desire against the Spirit, and the Spirit against the flesh; for these are in opposition to one another, so that you may not do the things that you please. But if you are led by the Spirit, you are not under the Law. Now the deeds of the flesh are evident, which are: immorality, impurity, sensuality, idolatry, sorcery, enmities, strife, jealousy, outbursts of anger, disputes, dissensions, factions, envying, drunkenness, carousing, and things like these, of which I forewarn you just as I have forewarned you that those who practice such things shall not inherit the kingdom of God.* (NASB)

As I look over the lists of fleshly passions, I notice that greed isn't listed. However Ephesians 5:3 ties greed right in with impurity. Leviticus 19:11 takes care of lying and stealing also. There just isn't any wiggle room for me to indulge myself in the things that the world has approved. The world gives lip service to avoiding many of these things but sexual promiscuity (including impurity) and carousing are probably the two most "tolerated" sins I see in society. I also find it interesting that sorcery and idolatry are listed in the deeds of the flesh. Both of these are becoming more commonplace.

What exactly is Peter talking about when he mentions the flesh? Some versions use the term sinful desires or sinful nature. The dictionary has a definition of flesh that explains it in secular terms: the physical body along with its needs and limitations, as opposed to the soul, mind, or spirit. There are limitations in me that are going to want to do the things listed. How can I abstain from these? The answer is in Galations 5:18. I must be lead by the Spirit. That means I must yield my desires and emotions (soul), my thinking that results in my goals (mind), and my body to God. Since my spirit has been born again, it is the only thing in me that is already yielded to God. It is the means by which the Holy Spirit lives in me and changes my desires to do God's will. Yielding is an ongoing process until one day I'll be completely submissive to God. That will be the day of His visitation (when Jesus returns again) or when I die and am finally with Him and free from all the temptations of the flesh.

Peter refers to the world as the Gentiles. Gentiles didn't have God's law and in the Jewish mind, they did all these things since they had no restraint. The world in Peter's era, for the most part, acknowledged that most of these things were wrong. Even today the world agrees, otherwise we wouldn't have everything from anger management classes to specific laws. This reveals that even a person who isn't being led by the Holy Spirit (a non-Christian) still has a sense of right and wrong.

When Jesus comes back again, it will be too late for non-Christians. However, they will still give glory to God. They will then have to admit that their accusations against us were false. I note, however, that they will do this because they will see my good deeds. One way of avoiding all the lusts of the flesh is to replace them with good deeds. Ephesians 4:25-32; 5:4, 11, and 17 lists sins and what I should do to replace those sins in my life. When I'm doing these things, the world will see and note it.

Don't be mistaken, the world knows how a Christian should behave even if they don't agree with us. Sometimes they know better than some Christians. They are watching and my strongest witness comes when my actions match my words.

Government – 1 Peter 2:13-14

Be subject for the Lord's sake to every human institution, whether it be to the emperor as supreme, or to governors as sent by him to punish those who do wrong and to praise those who do right. (RSV)

What a timely topic for an election day. I wrote it on Election Day in the U.S. It's too bad I didn't get it done sooner and post it on the web before or even on Tuesday.

It's hard for me to put together submission to human organizations in the same sentence with doing something for the Lord. But, there it is in black and white. The hard part of this is that Peter was writing to people who were persecuted by their government. It was written about 66 AD, which was two years before the end of Nero's reign of terror. He picked on Christians because they were easy targets and could divert attention away from his own political failings. I sometimes wonder how Peter could make this statement considering who was in power. However, it is evident that the power of the Holy Spirit was moving him to act justly and in accordance with the law of the land.

Of course we can point back to when Peter was called before the Jewish authority. Acts 4:18-20 *So they called them and charged them not to speak or teach at all in the name of Jesus. But Peter and John answered them, "Whether it is right in the sight of God to listen to you rather than to God, you must judge; for we cannot but speak of what we have seen and heard."* (RSV) This is probably the most often used passage used to disobey government edicts. It sets precedence for Christians everywhere to disobey the government when that law is violating God's commands. In my opinion, however, it does not give me the right to violate God's law in order to oppose the government.

In other words, I can't assassinate Nero because he has been wiping out Christians.

Romans 13:1-7 is Paul's comprehensive exposition on government. Take the time to look it up and read it. In it, Paul asserts that God establishes all governments. You can look back at the O.T. and see how God used ungodly rulers to punish Israel and Judah. He says that if I rebel against the government, I am likely to bring God's judgment on myself. Regardless of the government, I'm to do right because government is God's servant to bring wrath on the wrongdoer. This is not easy to hear, especially if I'm living under an oppressive government. Paul continues to say I must submit to that authority. I am to pay taxes because the government is God's servant who works full time governing.

I can understand why many Christians did not support the American Revolution. Their fellow citizens who wanted to break free from England ostracized them. However, they couldn't see any moral reason to rebel against the king. Taxation without representation was not a violation of God's commands in their eyes.

Today, I feel people who are creating and supporting initiatives to cut taxes are not looking at the big picture that Paul presented. They are only looking at their own pocketbook. There is a prevalent attitude among many that government is too big and should be scaled back. I believe that when Christians are not providing for the needs of others in the community, then the government has the right to tax us to provide those needs. I generally vote for levies because this is the means of paying for services that are beyond the Church's realm. Fire protection, police forces, public schools, libraries, roads, armed forces, you name it. The Church doesn't take care of these things with the possible exception of schools. However, there aren't enough Christian schools to take care of every child.

If I only pay taxes and don't get involved in any other way, then I shouldn't complain when the government is ungodly. 1 Timothy 2:1-2 *First of all, then, I urge that supplications, prayers, intercessions, and thanksgivings be made for all men, for kings and all who are in high positions, that we may lead a quiet and peaceable life, godly and respectful in every way.* (RSV) The first and foremost thing is to pray daily for our leaders, whether we like them or not. Titus 3:1-2 *Remind them to be submissive to rulers and authorities, to be obedient, to be ready for any honest work, to speak evil of no one, to avoid quarreling, to be gentle, and to show perfect courtesy toward all men.* (RSV) Included in that is not to continually bad-mouth our leaders. We should show perfect courtesy, not jumping up during a speech (or town meeting) and shouting insults.

Live Free – 1 Peter 2:15-17

For it is God's will that by doing right you should put to silence the ignorance of foolish men. Live as free men, yet without using your freedom as a pretext for evil; but live as servants of God. Honor all men. Love the brotherhood. Fear God. Honor the emperor. (RSV)

I have observed that doing right doesn't always silence the talk of foolish men in this world. I recently read an article on a very liberal web site which accused Christians of having an agenda to overtake the U.S. The means of doing this is by home schooling and private Christian schools. The claims are that Christians have been brainwashing the next generation and that we are the most dangerous of all factions. There was much name-calling in this article. The son of a well-known Christian theologian wrote it. He had been home schooled and advanced the very causes that he now rejects.[3]

So, in light of the current world, how am I to interpret these verses? I can only think this must refer back to verse 12 where Peter says that they will glorify God on the day of visitation. Certainly, Jesus predicted that we would be maligned and even worse. John 15:20-21 *"Remember the words I spoke to you: 'No servant is greater than his master.' If they persecuted me, they will persecute you also. If they obeyed my teaching, they will obey yours also. They will treat you this way because of my name, for they do not know the One who sent me."* (NIV®) I have a feeling that most foolish men will not be silenced until Jesus comes back.

In the meantime, I need to live as a free man. So what does that mean? Jesus said in John 8:31-36 that the truth will set me free. The Jews were shocked just as the people of the world are shocked at Christian behavior. They didn't consider themselves slaves just as

---

[3] http://www.huffingtonpost.com/frank-schaeffer/glenn-beck-and-the-912-ma_b_284387.html (Frank Schaeffer, Posted: September 12, 2009 04:37 PM)

non-Christians don't consider themselves as slaves to sin. But that is exactly what Jesus said.

So I need to live free from sin. Some read into Paul's writings that my freedom includes freedom from the Law and that is true. However I capitalized the word Law to limit its meaning to encompass the Levitical law of sacrifices and all that went with it. Regarding sin, Paul said in Romans 6:15 *What then? Shall we sin because we are not under law but under grace? By no means!* (NIV®) When I live free from sin and the law, I live by God's standards, which are even higher. That is why Peter added I must live as a servant of God.

In conclusion, this requires me to honor all men. It doesn't give me the right to abusive speech toward anyone in private or public. If someone is wrong, I can still point that out, not with name-calling, but with carefully researched truth.

I must also love the brotherhood – meaning that I am to love all Christians. I can't pick and choose which Christians I am to love based on their denomination. Again, that doesn't mean I have to condone heresy or bad doctrine that is taught in some denominations, but I am to love true believers.

Finally, I need to honor the king, emperor, president, prime minister, governor, mayor, or whoever is leading the country, state, city, or county. That means I need to treat them with the respect that is due their office. If they are in the wrong, I can still point it out, but in the same way as mentioned before.

Persecution or Stupidity – 1 Peter 2:18-20

Servants, you must respect your masters and do whatever they tell you-not only if they are kind and reasonable, but even if they are tough and cruel. Praise the Lord if you are punished for doing right! Of course, you get no credit for being patient if you are beaten for doing wrong; but if you do right and suffer for it, and are patient beneath the blows, God is well pleased. (TLB)

This must be one of the most quoted Bible verse for employer-employee relationships. Now that I'm self-employed, I only have one boss, Jesus. Well, actually I now work for several people – clients and customers. While working for a company, if I had thought of my employer as a customer for my services, there wouldn't be much difference.

Sometimes, a difficult part of working for others is telling them that what they are asking you to do isn't necessarily in their best interests. At these times, it can seem that they are not kind or reasonable. However, if I'm doing my best to do what is right, I'll have to trust the Lord that the end results will be good.

I'll digress a bit because many people use these verses to claim that they are suffering for Christ in the workplace when they are simply being punished for doing wrong. The usual complaint comes when a Christian shares some nuggets of faith with another co-worker or even a client during work time. The boss or other employees overhear or are the subject of the sharing and complain to management. The boss then reprimands the Christian for engaging in non-work activities and the Christian tells everyone that he or she is suffering for Christ.

Not so! I am not being paid to share Jesus with others during work time. I'm being paid to do my work. It doesn't matter that the person in the next cube or workstation is talking about last night's football game or anything else. It doesn't give me the right to steal time from my employer. The idea is that I have to live a life that will silence the talk of foolish men as Peter stated before.

So when can I share the Gospel with someone at work? There are breaks and lunch when you can do it if you are not violating common sense and company policy. It is one thing to know how to engage a person in spiritual conversations which lead to sharing Jesus, and it is another to buttonhole a person on break and back them into a corner. The first is Spirit-led and the second is worldly passion. Handing out tracts is usually against company policy – they consider that soliciting even though you aren't selling anything.

A side note. I checked this out with a local city office. I may pass out Christian literature without a solicitor's license as long as it doesn't ask anyone to buy something or attend an event with an admission price.

With all that said, there are laws that protect you at the workplace and you should know them as well. In general, your employer can't tell you not to wear Christian jewelry when others can wear jewelry. They can't prohibit you from having a Bible on your desk if others can have non-work related books. The same goes for mottos, calendars, and pictures.

In my work career, I only had one run-in with personnel over Christian witnessing. A co-worker and I were asked by another co-worker if we would talk to her about Christianity. We agreed and set up a time in the cafeteria during lunch. A few days later, my boss reprimanded me for proselytizing. My co-worker had the same conversation with her boss. We wracked our brains and realized that the lunchroom meeting was the only thing that could have been construed as proselytizing so we asked the woman if she had complained. She assured us that she hadn't.

Armed with that knowledge, we requested an audience with personnel and we were told we had violated company policy by trying to find out who had accused us, even though that person had not filed the complaint. At that point, I assured the personnel representative that I knew my rights and she had violated them by accusing us without proper investigation. That ended the matter and nothing was ever placed in my record or on my performance reviews. The person we shared with later discovered that a third party had reported us to her boss based on seeing us together in the lunchroom.

If, in that situation, we had been reprimanded, pay docked, or anything else, then we would have known that it pleased God. If we had really violated company policy in our attempts to witness, then God would not have been pleased.

I'm afraid that there are too many cases when Christians are poor workers or do stupid things and then claim to be suffering for Christ when they lose their jobs or are passed over for promotion. I pray that this happens less and less.

Called to Be Like Jesus – 1 Peter 2:21-23

To this you were called, because Christ suffered for you, leaving you an example, that you should follow in his steps. "He committed no sin, and no deceit was found in his mouth." When they hurled their insults at him, he did not retaliate; when he suffered, he made no threats. Instead, he entrusted himself to him who judges justly. (NIV®)

This is a continuation of the same thought as the previous section – suffering for doing right, not wrong. Obviously, Jesus is the prime example of suffering. I took a quick review of Jesus' "trial" and execution in John 18:19 – 20:30. It doesn't have all the details but it brings out enough to substantiate what Peter wrote.

I don't know if I would be able to be as trusting as Jesus was if I were thrown in prison then beaten for my faith. I'm pretty sure I would yell and scream at the beatings. I would make every effort to escape, but not by denying that I know Jesus. However, I have made up my mind that I would not seek my own revenge – I would not retaliate. I'm sure that if by some chance I had to stand trial or was asked to testify against my persecutors, I would tell the truth and not hold back in order to appear meek and humble. I don't think this is what Jesus would want nor is it what Peter was advocating.

There are many examples in the Gospels where Jesus went head to head with those who wanted to kill Him. Sometimes He answered them with parables as in Matthew 21:23-46. Sometimes He answered with Scriptural logic as in John 8:31-59, which ended when Jesus made an unmistakable claim to be God. As a result, His enemies started to stone Him. In that instance, He slipped away before they could harm Him. In Matthew 12:24-45 Jesus even called His detractors a brood of vipers and a wicked and adulterous generation. This doesn't seem to fit the mild, meek Jesus who Peter was describing. He even used a whip to chase merchants with evil intent from the temple. However, He never took up a sword to kill. He never resorted to physical violence to advance His cause or protect Himself or His disciples.

I think Peter was viewing the situation from the perspective Jesus described in Matthew 10:18-*20 "On my account you will be brought before governors and kings as witnesses to them and to the Gentiles. But when they arrest you, do not worry about what to say or how to say it. At that time you will be given what to say, for it will not be you speaking, but the Spirit of your Father speaking through you."* (NIV®) If I entrust myself to the Lord, then I can be confident that He will give the right words and the right actions when the time comes. If I do not trust Him, then I am very likely to be a bad witness for Jesus. It is very likely that I'll want my revenge. If I do, I will bring disgrace to the name of Christians everywhere. History has shown that when people who call themselves Christians (whether they are or not doesn't matter) do not take these passages to heart then the world eagerly points out their abuse and maligns the good name of Jesus.

There is no guarantee that I will be spared from persecutions. My brothers and sisters in Pakistan are currently facing an increase in persecution as the Taliban and other factions are increasing pressure on Christians. There has been more bloodshed, false imprisonment, and beatings. Matthew 24:9-*14 "Then they will deliver you up to tribulation, and put you to death; and you will be hated by all nations for my name's sake. And then many will fall away, and betray one another, and hate one another. And many false prophets will arise and lead many astray. And because wickedness is multiplied, most men's love will grow cold. But he who endures to the end will be saved. And this gospel of the kingdom will be preached throughout the whole world, as a testimony to all nations; and then the end will come."* (RSV) My prayer for them is that they will be able to be a testimony to those who watch and those who persecute. I pray that in their suffering, Jesus may be glorified, the ignorant talk of foolish men may be silenced, and that many will come to know Jesus. I pray that as a result of their hardship, the righteous Judge may find many more who call on the name of Jesus when He comes.

He Died For Me – 1 Peter 2:24-25

He himself bore our sins in his body on the tree, that we might die to sin and live to righteousness. By his wounds you have been healed. For you were straying like sheep, but have now returned to the Shepherd and Guardian of your souls. (RSV)

What did Jesus' suffering accomplish? When Jesus died on the cross (the tree), He fulfilled the requirement of the Law as a payment for sin. Deuteronomy 21:22-23 *If a man guilty of a capital offense is put to death and his body is hung on a tree, you must not leave his body on the tree overnight. Be sure to bury him that same day, because anyone who is hung on a tree is under God's curse. You must not desecrate the land the Lord your God is giving you as an inheritance.* (NIV®) Jesus took the curse of God's wrath (because of sin) on Himself. Over and over, it has been emphasized in the N.T. that Jesus was not guilty of any sin, yet He was executed. On the cross Jesus called out, asking why the Father had forsaken Him, indicating that God's wrath was truly on Him. If Jesus were not guilty, then why would the Father abandon Him? The answer can be only that my sin was placed on Him. 2 Corinthians 5:21 *For our sake he made him to be sin who knew no sin, so that in him we might become the righteousness of God.* (RSV)

How do I know that Jesus took my sin and that it was a satisfactory substitution for my death? I believe the resurrection of Jesus proves it. Jesus made many statements about eternal life and that it only comes through Him. John 5:24 *"Truly, truly, I say to you, he who hears my word and believes him who sent me, has eternal life; he does not come into judgment, but has passed from death to life."* John 14:6 *Jesus said to him, "I am the way, and the truth, and the life; no one comes to the Father, but by me."* (RSV) Remember, if Jesus had committed only one sin, then His death would have been the payment only for His own sin. He would not be able to pay for mine. If either of these two statements that Jesus made is false, then He was a liar and could not possibly pay for my sin. Since God did raise Jesus from the dead, it proves that everything Jesus said is true. It proves He and only He gives me eternal life so I can go to the Father also.

If there were any other way for me to obtain eternal life, then Jesus' death was a waste. Paul says in Galatians 3:21b-22 *For if a law had been given that could impart life, then righteousness would certainly have come by the law. But the Scripture declares that the whole world is a prisoner of sin, so that what was promised, being given through faith in Jesus Christ, might be given to those who believe.* (NIV®) He affirms, with Peter, that I am a sinner.

I went astray and now have come to Jesus, the Shepherd and Guardian of my soul. He who has saved me will guard me and keep me safe until the day He escorts me into the presence of the Father.

When Peter was writing these two short verses, He was either quoting from the O.T. or had it in mind. Read Isaiah 53: 4, 5, and 11. These verses are a vivid prediction of Jesus' suffering and atonement for my sin.

First Peter – Chapter Three

Husband – Wife Relationship – 1 Peter 3:1-7

In the same way, you wives, be submissive to your own husbands so that even if any of them are disobedient to the word, they may be won without a word by the behavior of their wives, as they observe your chaste and respectful behavior. And let not your adornment be merely external — braiding the hair, and wearing gold jewelry, or putting on dresses; but let it be the hidden person of the heart, with the imperishable quality of a gentle and quiet spirit, which is precious in the sight of God. For in this way in former times the holy women also, who hoped in God, used to adorn themselves, being submissive to their own husbands. Thus Sarah obeyed Abraham, calling him lord, and you have become her children if you do what is right without being frightened by any fear.

You husbands likewise, live with your wives in an understanding way, as with a weaker vessel, since she is a woman; and grant her honor as a fellow heir of the grace of life, so that your prayers may not be hindered. (NASB)

I wonder why Peter devoted six verses to wives and only one to husbands. My first thought is that he had to educate women about how dense guys are. Fallen man has a caveman mentality and lets his different biological makeup giving in to external visual stimulation. Christian men don't do much better when they don't put off their old self and put on the new self (Ephesians 4:22-24). Women need to understand that and not succumb to the temptation to attract men by external attraction instead of being obedient to the Word.

I've seen some sects which take these verses to mean women shouldn't do any of the things mentioned. The verses make no prohibition against outward adornment, but instead, point out that inward beauty will not only help improve their husband but is what pleases God.

The way the world is going now, guys have the same problem. Most think they have to be some kind of macho dude to get the chicks. However, if I develop character that pleases God, I will attract and have a spouse who has the same character. I hope my character pleases God, as I can testify that my wife attracted me with her hidden person of the heart before we were married.

I'll let a woman talk about what it means to be submissive to her husband. I need to concentrate on what I should be as a husband and leave that up to my wife. These verses make it clear that I need to understand my wife. I need to make every effort to know what she likes and dislikes. I need to know how to speak to her so she knows I love her and want the very best for her. I need to treat her with respect and gentleness. Men don't know their own strength and how easy it is to hurt their wives physically. Neither do they know how easy it is to hurt them emotionally. Then there are some jerks who take the submissive thing to the point that they want to control their wives, physically and emotionally. There is no room for that in the Christian walk. Peter warns me that my prayers will be hindered if I'm not treating my wife the way I should.

Ephesians 5:25-33 has the most comprehensive prescription for being a husband. A few points from those verses make it impossible to be perfect husband. There is no way I can love my wife with the same unconditional, unselfish love that Jesus has for us. It doesn't mean I don't try.

I'm to protect her purity. That means I have to be pure and stay away from any kind of pornography, sexual deviation, greed, idolatry, or any other sin.

Paul says that no one hates his own body but loves it. Some may argue that, especially with the high suicide rate, a person is trying to do what they think is best for their body by escaping from the torment or pain through which they are going. Regardless, Paul is using this to make sure I know I need to give my wife the same attention I give myself.

Harmony – 1 Peter 3:8-9

Finally, all of you, live in harmony with one another; be sympathetic, love as brothers, be compassionate and humble. Do not repay evil with evil or insult with insult, but with blessing, because to this you were called so that you may inherit a blessing. (NIV®)

It seems quite simple and straightforward to me. The commands are clear and easy to understand. At the beginning of the verses are the ways I should act towards other. It is followed by how I should respond to people who don't follow these rules. Then there is the reward for doing it. Ok, next section. Well, maybe not. If it were that easy, I'm sure there would be less conflict in churches and the world in general. Doing these things is a lot harder than knowing I should do them.

Romans 12:16 *Live in harmony with one another. Do not be proud, but be willing to associate with people of low position. Do not be conceited.* (NIV®) I need to address pride and conceit in myself if I actually want to live in harmony. I can't be proud. I looked this up in the dictionary[4] and it didn't sound so bad. (Pride: the happy satisfied feeling somebody experiences when having or achieving something special that other people admire. Something such as an achievement or possession that somebody feels especially pleased and satisfied with.) Hmmm, shouldn't I feel good about getting something done? That doesn't sound so bad. However, I can see that pride of ownership can cause problems, especially when it makes others who don't have the same things feel out of place or inferior. That's a good one to work on. I don't want to let my possessions cause others to be intimidated or feel I think less of them.

Another definition of proud is arrogant (having an exaggerated opinion of personal worth or abilities). Other versions of the Bible use the word haughty instead of proud. It comes from the Greek word *hupselos* (hoop-say-los') which means loft (in place or character). That seems to fit better, especially in context with the part about being willing to associate with people of low position. I don't want to appear to be above them or anyone else. Romans 12:3 says that I should not think of myself more highly than I ought. Remembering that it is only by the blood of Jesus that I'm in God's grace and not because of my own worth is a good way to help me from being proud, arrogant, or haughty.

It is also good to acknowledging God's sovereignty. I didn't choose where I was born, who my parents were, or any of my natural abilities. I remember talking to a man who was offended when I suggested that he wasn't in control of his life. He assured me he had worked hard for his wonderful house, job, education, and everything

---

[4] Encarta® World English Dictionary [North American Edition] © & (P)2009 Microsoft Corporation.

he had. When I asked him if he chose where he was born or that he was born to white middle class parents, he essentially asked what that had to do with anything. He didn't get it. Lord, help me to always acknowledge that everything I am and have comes from You!

Don't repay evil for evil, etc. I think I've already gone over that. If not, this proverb says a lot. Proverbs 19:11 *A man's wisdom gives him patience; it is to his glory to overlook an offense.* (NIV®) If I don't overlook offenses, I'm pretty stupid. I want to do what pleases God and He says I'll be rewarded when I overlook offences. It takes patience to do that and shows my wisdom or lack of it when I lose it. It's hard, in the middle of a life situation, to keep my mouth from blurting out hurtful things before I think about them. That's why it takes practice to hold my tongue. Psalm 141:3 *Set a guard over my mouth, O Lord, keep watch over the door of my lips!* (RSV) It also takes a dependence on the Holy Spirit.

Having the right attitude toward others and not seeking revenge will provide for me an inheritance that won't fade or spoil. These are the treasures I can store up in heaven.

Clean Heart – 1 Peter 3:10-12

For, "Whoever would love life and see good days must keep his tongue from evil and his lips from deceitful speech. He must turn from evil and do good; he must seek peace and pursue it. For the eyes of the Lord are on the righteous and his ears are attentive to their prayer, but the face of the Lord is against those who do evil." (NIV®)

Deuteronomy 32:46-47 speaks of the very words that God gave to the Israelites just before they entered the Promised Land. He said that if they took His words to heart and taught them to their children, they would enjoy long life. He said that the words were not idle but were their life. Do I treat God's Word as my life? Is it the most important part of my life? If so, then I will be diligent to teach my children. My kids are grown and I have grandchildren. I tried to teach them as they grew up and now they are doing the same with their kids. That is a joy to see.

Part of taking God's words to heart includes keeping my tongue from evil and deceitful speech. Peter is quoting Psalm 34:12-16. In it,

God has given us a very simple formula for living a good life. The first part involves the heart and mind. Jesus said in Matthew 15:18-20 that what comes out of my mouth reveals what is in my heart. If my heart is harboring evil, then I will naturally speak evil. I won't be able to stop it. Using my own will power, I can attempt to keep my speech clean and even succeed, however it will sneak out at the most inopportune time. The only way to resolve that problem is to ask God for a clean heart.

Psalm 51:10-12 *Create in me a clean heart, O God, and put a new and right spirit within me. Cast me not away from thy presence, and take not thy holy Spirit from me. Restore to me the joy of thy salvation, and uphold me with a willing spirit.* (RSV) The only way to have a clean mouth is to have a clean heart and mind. With the power of His Holy Spirit, I can speak in the way He wants. I can build others up according to their needs and not tear them down (Ephesians 4:29).

The second part of taking God's word to heart is to it into practice. It doesn't do any good to conform to correct speech without physically following through. "Put your money where your mouth is." If I say the right things, but by my actions convey a different attitude, then I haven't let God cleanse my heart. I haven't submitted to Him if I don't actually do what He says. James 1:22 *Do not merely listen to the word, and so deceive yourselves. Do what it says.* (NIV®) I can actually listen to God's word and deceive myself by thinking that by simply knowing His Word, it is going to save or change me.

God listens to me when I have actually submitted to Him and He then gives me a clean heart. Does that mean He gives me everything I want in prayer? No, it means that He works everything for my good (Rom 8:28), even the bad things that happen. I can't toss all the other verses in 1Peter and assume everything is going to be roses all the time. However, I can rest assured that the God of the universe, the Creator of all things, He who controls all things, has my best interests at heart. I may not see the results until I reach heaven, but I know it will all make sense then.

This same God and Father who loves me has not promised good for those who do not love Him. The Psalms say quite the opposite. His face is against the unrighteous. In fact, the Bible says a lot about the outcome of those who do not love God. Hebrews 10:*31 It is a dreadful thing to fall into the hands of the living God.* (NIV®)

There is a simple test to determine if I really love God. John 14:21 *"Whoever has my commands and obeys them, he is the one who loves me. He who loves me will be loved by my Father, and I too will love him and show myself to him."* (NIV®) So what are these commands that Jesus says I need to obey? 1 John 4:20-21 *If any one says, "I love God," and hates his brother, he is a liar; for he who does not love his brother whom he has seen, cannot love God whom he has not seen. And this commandment we have from him, that he who loves God should love his brother also.* (RSV)

The Hope That I Have – 1 Peter 3:13-17

Who is going to harm you if you are eager to do good? But even if you should suffer for what is right, you are blessed. "Do not fear what they fear; do not be frightened." But in your hearts set apart Christ as Lord. Always be prepared to give an answer to everyone who asks you to give the reason for the hope that you have. But do this with gentleness and respect, keeping a clear conscience, so that those who speak maliciously against your good behavior in Christ may be ashamed of their slander. It is better, if it is God's will, to suffer for doing good than for doing evil. (NIV®)

Peter knew full well that Christians were being harmed for no reason. They were trying to do good, yet they were being persecuted. This still happens today as it has happened in the past. David ran into this problem. Psalm 38:20 *Those who repay my good with evil slander me when I pursue what is good.* (NIV®) Jesus warned us that it would happen to us simply because we belong to Him. John 15:18 *"If the world hates you, know that it has hated me before it hated you."* (RSV) The main reason is that when we do good, it reminds others they are not in a right standing with God. They therefore want to remove anything that convicts them. John 15:22-23 *"If I had not come and spoken to them, they would not have sin; but now they have no excuse for their sin. He who hates me hates my Father also."* (RSV)

I realize how intolerant it is to tell or show someone the errors of their ways. Today, everything is a matter of one's own judgment. Therefore I deserve to be ostracized or even worse if I point out certain behavior is actually wrong based on an absolute standard that is not within my own judgment, i.e. God's. However, aren't others being intolerant of my belief? The only way I can suffer for what is right and know I'm doing right is to have a standard that supersedes what others believe to be right based on their own desires and dreams.

What do "they" fear? Most people fear death more than anything else. That is most often the threat of severe persecutors. They believe that under the threat of death, Christians will recant their faith. It burns them to no end when it doesn't work. It only makes them madder and they often carry out their threats.

How can I not be frightened under those circumstances? By setting apart Christ as Lord in my heart. If I really believe Him, then death is not the worst thing that can happen to me. Revelation 1:17-18 *When I saw him, I fell at his feet as though dead. Then he placed his right hand on me and said: "Do not be afraid. I am the First and the Last. I am the Living One; I was dead, and behold I am alive for ever and ever! And I hold the keys of death and Hades."* (NIV®) When I belong to Jesus, I am promised eternal life. Jesus rose from the dead and defeated death. He now holds the key to death so that when I die, I'll be brought into eternal life and live with Him forever. With that view, the threats to succumb to the world's standards of right and wrong are pure foolishness. The temptations to live life for today and worldly pleasures are overcome by the knowledge that something far better awaits me.

This is the hope I have. The tough part is letting others know about it with humility and respect. I've been accused of being arrogant because I know where I'm going and most people don't think anyone can know that. But that is what God's Word tells me. 1 John 5:13 *I write this to you who believe in the name of the Son of God, that you may know that you have eternal life.* (RSV)

Sometimes I just want to thump a person on the head and yell, "Wake up!" (Not very respectful.) Many people have their own ideas of who God is. Their ideas are based on their own wishful thinking. They somehow think God thinks and acts just like they do so they do as they please. Psalm 50:21 *These things you have done and I kept silent; you thought I was altogether like you. But I will rebuke you and accuse you to your face.* (NIV®) Even though God will rebuke and punish them for those ideas and actions, they think it is totally wrong for me to warn them. They've heard Jesus is the only way to God and they don't like it. The excuses are plentiful – everything from thinking Jesus didn't really mean that, to simply ignoring it and saying they believe there are many roads to heaven. Don't they know there are many roads to hell and only one to heaven? They have the same excuses for ignoring that as well.

So they slander Christians as being intolerant, along with other things. However, they will still see the good things I do and realize that they are wrong even if they don't want to admit it.

Yeah, there are some who call themselves Christians and do some pretty horrific things. Sooner or later, they will suffer for their wrongs. Some claim to be martyrs but the truth is they are getting what they deserve. But that's not where I want to be and it isn't where God wants me or anyone else to be.

Once for All – 1 Peter 3:18

For Christ also died for sins once for all, the righteous for the unrighteous, that he might bring us to God, being put to death in the flesh but made alive in the spirit; (RSV)

Jesus died once for all people and that includes me. I think this is one of the greatest statements in the Bible. It is used six other times to explain Jesus died only once and His one-time death was a sacrifice for all of my sins. His one-time shedding of His blood was sufficient to provide me with eternal redemption. His sacrifice has done away with sin once for all, meaning that it works forward in time from His death as well as backward. He doesn't have to die each day to cover my sins committed from one day to the next. His one-time death is able to cleanse my conscience from guilt because that death is able to make me holy. See Romans 6:10, Hebrews 7:27, 9:12, 9:26, 10:2, and 10:10.

You will note I used the words "is able" a couple of times. I used those words because not everyone is cleansed from guilt, given eternal life, or made holy. Only those who accept this and turn to Jesus in repentance of their sins will have this forgiveness and the rewards. God didn't automatically forgive everyone on the earth when He accepted Jesus' sacrifice for sin. Just like the people in the O.T. who had to come before God and lay their hands on the goat or lamb, which was about to be slaughtered, and confess their sins, so I also had to do that in a symbolic way. I couldn't physically put my hands on Jesus' head and transfer my sins to Him in the same symbolic way. So God had to do it. 2 Corinthians 5:21 *God made him who had no sin to be sin for us, so that in him we might become the righteousness of God.* (NIV®) However, it wasn't until I confessed my sin and turned from it that I could claim to be forgiven and obtain the righteousness He provided.

Being made holy or righteous must sound really radical, weird, arrogant, and /or cultish to someone who hasn't turned to Jesus. Yes, Jesus has made me holy. It isn't as if I've achieved perfection or even claim to be perfect though. His declaration that I'm holy simply means I'm forgiven and when I stand before God, Jesus' holiness will be seen and not mine. It also means that from now on, I'm being made holy – day-by-day I'm being cleaned up, one sinful habit and slipup after another. It's a lifetime endeavor and won't be completed until I reach heaven.

Before I came to know Jesus, I believed the whole death and resurrection of Jesus was an elaborate hoax. I knew all the theories that people have used to try to explain why He either didn't really die or that He didn't really rise from the dead. A careful reading of the Gospels reproves each of the theories.

He didn't really die. Hogwash! He was scourged and many people died during that ordeal. He was almost at the point of death and then nailed to the cross. Witnesses saw Him die. The Roman soldiers, who were experts at crucifying people, testified that He was dead. The blood and water that poured from His side proved He was already dead because it showed His blood had already separated into components. Joseph and Nicodemus took His body and wrapped it in 75 pounds of spices and cloth. Can you imagine how Jesus could have survived that? Can you imagine two of His followers doing that if He were still alive?

He wasn't raised but His body was stolen by His disciples. Yeah, sure, if you believe that, I have a bridge I want to sell you. You really expect His wimpy disciples who ran away when Jesus was arrested would mount an attack on the Roman guards? These guards lost a body; by Roman custom, they should have been executed for failure to carry out a simple mission. Why weren't they? There is only one explanation. Matthew 28:12-15 *When the chief priests had met with the elders and devised a plan, they gave the soldiers a large sum of money, telling them, "You are to say, 'His disciples came during the night and stole him away while we were asleep.' If this report gets to the governor, we will satisfy him and keep you out of trouble." So the soldiers took the money and did as they were instructed. And this story has been widely circulated among the Jews to this very day.* (NIV®) By the way, Roman guards don't fall asleep while on duty – another possible death sentence. The guards had the money to escape punishment and the story is still being told to our generation.

Some complain and say that if Jesus was God and God died then how can He raise Himself? The 1 Peter verse says He was made alive by the Spirit. So the whole Trinity thing comes into play here. Do I understand how God can be three Persons in one God? No, not really. I simply have to go on the fact that Jesus said He was God and the Spirit is mentioned throughout the Bible, O.T. and N.T. As early as Genesis 1:26 and 11:7, God revealed His triune nature when He said, "Let Us…" Since we can't really understand God, we have to take it on faith that He is triune, that He could empty Himself of His God nature and become a man (Philippians 2:6-7). If He can do that, then Jesus could really die and the Spirit could make Him alive again.

Trinity – 1 Peter 3:18b-20a Part I

He was put to death in the body but made alive by the Spirit, through whom also he went and preached to the spirits in prison who disobeyed long ago when God waited patiently in the days of Noah while the ark was being built. (NIV®)

I had to take the last part of verse 18 and the first of 20 to get one whole sentence. This last paragraph in chapter three is very interesting because of the many different subjects in it. For instance, I mentioned the Trinity in my last writing and commented that Jesus is God. Since it was not the main topic, I didn't pursue it further. However, I have studied it quite thoroughly and can with all conviction say that Jesus is indeed the Almighty God. One of the reminders of Jesus being God is found every Christmas. Isaiah 9:6 *For to us a child is born, to us a son is given, and the government will be on his shoulders. And he will be called Wonderful Counselor, Mighty God, Everlasting Father, Prince of Peace.* (NIV®) The triune nature of God is clearly seen in this passage. The Son is called the Wonderful Counselor, who is the Holy Spirit. He is called the Mighty God and Everlasting Father. Now who else can that be other than God the Father? He is called Prince of Peace – the Son.

What did Jesus have to say of Himself? John 10:30 *"I and the Father are one."* (NIV®) Did Jesus mean that He is one only in purpose (as some claim) or did He mean more when He said that? Let the people who heard Him explain what He meant. John 10:33 *"We are not stoning you for any of these,"* replied the Jews, *"but for blasphemy, because you, a mere man, claim to be God."* (NIV®) The Jews knew exactly what Jesus meant. Now, if I made a statement like that and someone misunderstood me, I would quickly clarify they misunderstood and there would be no problem. Did Jesus try to correct their understanding? Not at all. Read the next few verses and you will see they still tried to kill Him.

Still skeptical about the fact Jesus claimed to be God? How about John 8:58-59 *"I tell you the truth,"* Jesus answered, *"before Abraham was born, I am!" At this, they picked up stones to stone him, but Jesus hid himself, slipping away from the temple grounds.* (NIV®) Jesus used the words *"I am"* to convey clearly that He is God and that He has always existed as God, even before Abraham was born. Again, the Jews, who knew exactly what he meant, tried to stone Him for these comments.

Jesus made it clear God is the only one to be worshiped. Matthew 4:*10 Jesus said to him, "Away from me, Satan! For it is written: 'Worship the Lord your God, and serve him only.'"* (NIV®) I would think it strange that Jesus would say this, then later accept worship if He were not God. Matthew 28:9 *Suddenly Jesus met them. "Greetings," he said. They came to him, clasped his feet and worshiped him.* (NIV®) Did Jesus rebuke these women for worshiping Him? Not at all. When Thomas called Jesus his Lord and God in John 20:28, did Jesus correct him? Not at all. Did Thomas say God but not mean the Almighty God? There is nothing in the passage or the original language that suggests anything else, contrary to what some would say.

If Jesus were not God, then He has committed a sin that is the same as one which caused Satan's downfall. He has accepted worship and called Himself God. What happened to Herod when he let people simply call him a god? Acts 12:21-23 *On the appointed day Herod, wearing his royal robes, sat on his throne and delivered a public address to the people. They shouted, "This is the voice of a god, not of a man." Immediately, because Herod did not give praise to God, an angel of the Lord struck him down, and he was eaten by worms and died.* (NIV®) How much more would God not approve of someone who claimed to be God and accepted worship.

One thing is for sure, if Jesus were not God but claimed to be God, if He were not God and accepted worship, the resurrection would have never happened. Jesus would have died for His own sins and His death on the cross would have no meaning for me or anyone else. His disciples would have disbanded and the name of Jesus would only be a minor blip in history. However, repeatedly in the Bible, Jesus is upheld as sinless. His sinless death bought my redemption. If He were sinful then His death could not purchase my pardon. He is upheld as God by Christians around the world in spite of those who would try to minimize Him and thus play into Satan's hands. If you believe Jesus is not God, then you believe in a Jesus who is not able to save you from your sins. If you are not saved from your sins, then there is only one eternal outcome and it isn't good.

Either Jesus has to be God or He has to be a blasphemer or a lunatic. If He were either of the latter two then there is no way He should be followed, just as Jim Jones and other lunatic cult leaders should not be followed, let alone worshiped. On the other hand, if He is God, then I need to bow down and worship Him along with those through history who have affirmed He is God and there is no other name under heaven by which I can be saved (Acts 4:12).

No Second Chance – 1 Peter 3:18b-20a Part II

He was put to death in the body but made alive by the Spirit, through whom also he went and preached to the spirits in prison who disobeyed long ago when God waited patiently in the days of Noah while the ark was being built. (NIV®)

Now that I've stated my belief that Jesus is God and some more on the Trinity, I'll move on to the next topic and that is all this stuff about Jesus preaching to the spirits in prison. The first thing to note is that it was Jesus who preached to them but He did it through the Spirit who made Him alive. All I can say is that it is further proof God is triune. If I can say Jesus is God and the Spirit is God, then I can also say Jesus is the Spirit. Ephesians 3:17 *and that Christ may dwell in your hearts through faith;* (RSV) 1 Corinthians 3:16 *Do you not know that you are God's temple and that God's Spirit dwells in you?* (RSV) In one verse I can see Jesus lives in me by faith. In the next verse, I can see that the Holy Spirit lives in me. Since Jesus, the Holy Spirit, and God are all one, then it means I have all the fullness of God living in me (Ephesians 3:19). I have Jesus, the Holy Spirit, and the Father.

Some want to split hairs and say you must receive Jesus, then you must receive the Holy Spirit. Others say that you then must receive the Father. If you have only Jesus, then you aren't a full-fledged Christian. Hogwash! If you have one, you have all three. Of course, if the Jesus I received isn't God, then I've received an imitation and imitations have their limits. The biggest limitation is that no imitation Jesus is able to save me.

How do I figure out who these spirits in prison are? One clue would be what Peter writes in the next chapter. 1 Peter 4:6 *For this is why the gospel was preached even to the dead, that though judged in the flesh like men, they might live in the spirit like God.* (RSV) Jesus preached to those who are dead. If they are dead that implies they are people and not just spirits like angels or fallen angels. I assume that spirits can't die. Peter again mentions the judgment during Noah's time. 2 Peter 2:5 *if he did not spare the ancient world, but preserved Noah, a herald of righteousness, with seven other persons, when he brought a flood upon the world of the ungodly;* (RSV) I had read this in the NIV® before and it says that God brought the flood on the world's ungodly people. The Greek doesn't say people, it says world. So I went back to the O.T. to see what it says about the flood.

Genesis 6:5 *Then the Lord saw that the wickedness of man was great on the earth, and that every intent of the thoughts of his heart was only evil continually.* Genesis 6:8 *Noah was a righteous man, blameless in his time; Noah walked with God.* Genesis 6:12 *And God looked on the earth, and behold, it was corrupt; for all flesh had corrupted their way upon the earth.* (NASB) According to the original account, there was only one person whom God saw as blameless – Noah. From this I can determine that everyone who died in the flood was a sinner and deserved the fate of death, for the wages of sin is death (Romans 6:23). All this just to find out that the people Jesus is preaching to are ungodly, not demons who have fallen.

1 Peter 4:6 is tough to get my head around. First, because I normally think of ungodly dead people in a sort of never-never land

where they aren't aware of anything until the final judgment comes. This verse implies they are aware and that when Jesus went to them they could understand what He told them. Luke 16:19-31 also supports the idea they know what is going on and are conscious. 2 Peter 2:*9 then the Lord knows how to rescue the godly from trial, and to keep the unrighteous under punishment until the day of judgment,* (RSV) implies the same thing. Not only are they aware but they are being punished even while they await judgment.

The second thing about 1 Peter 4:6 is that it implies there might be some sort of second chance for them, if not for all who die without Christ. Just what does the phrase mean, *"they might live in the spirit like God."*? Does it mean a second chance for salvation or does it mean something else? Is there a possibility of a second chance? The Greek word for "like" is *"kata"* and the definition doesn't help. It is "down from, through out, according to, toward, along." In the KJV it is translated "according" in this verse and differently in some 40 other places it is used. Most translations use "according" in this verse so it says they will live according to God in the spirit. I think this simply means that even a person who dies without Christ has eternal life. Unfortunately that doesn't mean they are with God, but according to other Scriptures, too numerous to mention here, they will live in eternal torment with no way out.

The preaching Jesus provided may very well have gone like this, "You thought because so many rebelled that I would forgive you. You thought since no one could live a holy life and please my Father that I would have to let you off the hook. Well, I've come to tell you that I emptied myself of my God-nature and became a man. I lived a holy life proving it can be done. I paid the penalty of death for all who would believe in me and turn to me for salvation. However, you turned away from my Father and did not repent when you were confronted by Noah. By turning away from my Father, you rejected me. Therefore, your condemnation stands. There is no second chance after death."

This is not a very uplifting study. However, it does serve as a warning. The same applies today. If I have Jesus, I have eternal life apart from eternal punishment. If I don't, and die, there is no second chance. Today is the day to decide to follow Jesus.

Does Baptism Save Me? – 1 Peter 3:20b-22

In it [the ark] only a few people, eight in all, were saved through water, and this water symbolizes baptism that now saves you also — not the removal of dirt from the body but the pledge of a good conscience toward God. It saves you by the resurrection of Jesus Christ, who has gone into heaven and is at God's right hand — with angels, authorities and powers in submission to him. (NIV®)

It is evident from these verses that baptism, all by itself, can't save me. I am saved when I have the right attitude, i.e., a pledge of a good conscience toward God. A good conscience toward God means that I must believe He exists and that He rewards those who seek Him (Hebrews 11:6). It also means that if someone comes to me and says I need to be baptized in order to be saved and if I jump in the water but don't care about pleasing God or being submission to Him, then I won't be saved at all. Outward obedience to a command of God without a heartfelt desire to live for Him isn't worth anything. This is what God said to the Israelites through Isaiah the prophet. Isaiah 29:13-15 *And the Lord said: "Because this people draw near with their mouth and honor me with their lips, while their hearts are far from me, and their fear of me is a commandment of men learned by rote; therefore, behold, I will again do marvelous things with this people, wonderful and marvelous; and the wisdom of their wise men shall perish, and the discernment of their discerning men shall be hid." Woe to those who hide deep from the Lord their counsel, whose deeds are in the dark, and who say, "Who sees us? Who knows us?"* (RSV)

Baptism doesn't save me if I don't acknowledge Jesus is God, which is proven by His resurrection. If I don't believe He is sitting at the right hand of God, baptism is worthless.

Baptism wasn't invented by Christians. It was around a long time before Jesus came on the scene. Most thought that if they followed ceremonial cleansing, they would become acceptable to God. They thought doing the right stuff would earn their right to eternal life. They were wrong. John the Baptist was on the right track when he was baptizing people to get them ready for Jesus. Matthew 3:11 *"As for me, I baptize you with water for repentance, but He who is coming after me is mightier than I, and I am not fit to remove His sandals; He will baptize you with the Holy Spirit and fire."* (NASB) John's baptism didn't save anyone as was made evident later. However, the outward sign of baptism indicating repentance will save me because I have a desire to submit to God.

When I look at all that must accompany baptism to be saved, it becomes apparent baptism is not the vehicle or the necessary ingredient for salvation. Rather it becomes an outward demonstration of what has already occurred in the heart of a believer. Baptism should be one of the first steps of obedience by a person who has repented and changed his mind about sin and who God is. I have to confess it took me seven years after becoming a Christian to be baptized. I would argue with people who said I didn't have the Holy Spirit and wasn't a true believer because I hadn't been baptized. I knew beyond a shadow of a doubt I was saved because the Holy Spirit let me know (1 John 3:24, 4:13). I also realized they were teaching a false doctrine because they would also say, only after I interrogated them, that the baptism was only valid if it was done in their church.

However, my attitude changed when I heard a preacher talk about baptism from Romans 6:3-7. *Or don't you know that all of us who were baptized into Christ Jesus were baptized into his death? We were therefore buried with him through baptism into death in order that, just as Christ was raised from the dead through the glory of the Father, we too may live a new life. If we have been united with him like this in his death, we will certainly also be united with him in his resurrection. For we know that our old self was crucified with him so that the body of sin might be done away with, that we should no longer be slaves to sin— because anyone who has died has been freed from sin.* (NIV®) I was convicted that I must completely identify with Jesus in His death in order to live a new life in complete victory over sin. He also used Matthew 28:19-20. The Great Commission says that as a believer, I need to baptize followers if they are to be disciples. How could I baptize others if I refused to be baptized? It was a point of obedience to Jesus' command. Since I was disobeying Him in this simple act, how could I tell others to obey Him? If I was disobeying Him at this point, I was leaving myself vulnerable to Satan's attacks. In essence, by ignoring baptism, I was not identifying with Jesus in His death and I was therefore still a slave to the blatant sin of disobedience.

Just to be clear, a person can be saved without baptism. In fact, baptism never occurred in the Bible until someone made some profession of faith. So a person is saved before they are baptized. The thief on the cross never had an opportunity to be baptized but was saved, just as Jesus said. Don't tell me he was an exception. He was an example. In Acts 2:41, those who received the word were baptized. They believed first. Acts 10:48 clearly showed that the Gentiles had received the Holy Spirit before being baptized. They weren't exceptions either, but examples.

Acts 19:5 is an example of people who had been baptized but didn't know about Jesus. They only had John's baptism. They weren't saved until they had the right details, the correct knowledge. Faith in the wrong things doesn't save.

All the comments about the need to have the right heart attitude and to believe before being baptized leads to one other conclusion. Infant baptism or baptizing children who are not capable of making a decision to follow Jesus is not going to save them. When I mention this to people who believe the opposite, they point to Acts 16:33 where the jailer and all his household or family was baptized. First of all, the verse does not say infants were baptized. We have no way of knowing whether or not the jailer had babies in his family at that time. To imply that infants were baptized is making the verse say something it doesn't. In addition, the word household or family is not in the original Greek text. The NASB italicizes "household" to indicate that it is a word that has been added in translation. The Greek simply says he and his all were baptized.

Don't make the false assumption that because you were baptized as an infant you have a ticket to heaven. I was, but saw my need for salvation as an adult. Don't make the false assumption that because your babies have been baptized they have a ticket to heaven either. You need to make sure they know the way as soon as they can understand.

How to Be Great and Who Are Those Guys? – 1 Peter 3:22

Who [Jesus Christ] has gone into heaven and is at the right hand of God, with angels, authorities, and powers subject to him. (RSV)

How to Be Great

What does it mean to be sitting at the right hand of God? The right hand man of a king or any other authority is the person who is in charge of the daily affairs of the kingdom or company. Good examples are Joseph, Daniel, and Mordecai in the O.T. Each of these men became second in command to the king after he proved himself capable. The king didn't have to worry because these honest men were not looking out for their own good, but the good of the kingdom. In the same way, Jesus always sought to glorify the Father by doing His will. John 4:34 *"My food," said Jesus, "is to do the will of him who sent me and to finish his work."* (NIV®)

How does this apply to me? Philippians 2:3-7 *Do nothing out of selfish ambition or vain conceit, but in humility consider others better than yourselves. Each of you should look not only to your own interests, but also to the interests of others. Your attitude should be the same as that of Christ Jesus: Who, being in very nature God, did not consider equality with God something to be grasped, but made himself nothing, taking the very nature of a servant, being made in human likeness.* (NIV®) This is the secret to greatness, putting others first. Jesus sat down at the right hand of God because He put us first. He gave up everything to serve us. Once He accomplished that, He was exalted to the highest position in heaven that can be attained (Ephesians 1:21-22). Everything was put under His dominion and control. This doesn't mean I will attain to the same position as Jesus if I seek the welfare of others above my own. There is only one place in heaven with that authority and Jesus has it. However, I will have a position of authority in heaven. Revelation 1:5b-6 *To him who loves us and has freed us from our sins by his blood, and has made us to be a kingdom and priests to serve his God and Father — to him be glory and power for ever and ever! Amen.* (NIV®) As I serve as a priest in the kingdom of Jesus, I'll bring glory to the Father. Since this is Jesus' goal, it is mine as well.

Who Are Those Guys?

Who are these angels, authorities, and powers who are subject to Jesus? Angels are pretty easy to identify. Hebrews 1:14 *Are not all angels ministering spirits sent to serve those who will inherit salvation?* (NIV®) They are clearly beings who are the good guys. They do what God wants them to do, every time and without fail.

The authorities and powers are not as easy to identify since they are represented as evil in various places. Ephesians 6:11-12 *Put on the full armor of God so that you can take your stand against the devil's schemes. For our struggle is not against flesh and blood, but against the rulers, against the authorities, against the powers of this dark world and against the spiritual forces of evil in the heavenly realms.* (NIV®) In these verses, they are clearly aligned with the devil and his schemes.

Daniel gave us a very brief and mysterious glimpse into this spiritual world. Daniel 10:20-21 *Then he said, "Do you know why I have come to you? But now I will return to fight against the prince of Persia; and when I am through with him, lo, the prince of Greece will come. But I will tell you what is inscribed in the book of truth: there is none who contends by my side against these except Michael, your prince.* (RSV) In these verses, I can see that there are both good and evil powers and principalities. I can imagine that in the spiritual realms, there are beings who exercise some sort of power or control over the leaders and peoples of nations. As this angel (Gabriel) fought against the prince of Persia, I can imagine he was able to restrain the prince of Persia from eradicating the Jews who were in exile. You can read the book of Esther to see what that struggle looked like on the human level. I can only imagine what it looked like in the heavenly realm.

Elisha could see these mighty battles and prayed to let his servant see what was happening behind the scenes. 2 Kings 6:17 *And Elisha prayed, "O Lord, open his eyes so he may see." Then the Lord opened the servant's eyes, and he looked and saw the hills full of horses and chariots of fire all around Elisha.* (NIV®) Elisha prayed the physical enemy would be blinded and they were so he could lead them captive to the king of Israel. I'm positive that the surrounding angelic army caused Elisha's enemies to be blinded.

So it seems each nation has an evil prince who seeks to destroy and a holy one, an angel, who seeks to protect. Satan told Jesus that all the kingdoms of the earth belonged to him and Jesus didn't deny it (Matthew 4:8-9.) At this time, Satan is still in control of the nations (Ephesians 2:2) even though Jesus has been seated as the authority over all. One day Jesus will come back and take full control of the earth. That is when we will reign with him. Revelation 20:6 *Blessed and holy is he who shares in the first resurrection! Over such the second death has no power, but they shall be priests of God and of Christ, and they shall reign with him a thousand years.* (RSV)

In the meantime, when bad things happen I know that my Lord Jesus is in ultimate control. Satan may think he is ruling but I know he can do no more than Jesus allows (Job 1:6-12, 2:1-6.) I can be confident in the following verse. Romans 8:28 *We know that in everything God works for good with those who love him, who are called according to his purpose.* (RSV) Those who are not under Jesus' authority, who have not submitted to Him, can't claim this verse. When Jesus comes back, they will find themselves on the wrong side and will be punished for eternity.

I'm glad I know I'm on the right side. I didn't join Jesus for all the benefits. I've only learned about them as I study the Bible. It turns out that believers are blessed with much more than we can understand even after a lifetime of study.

First Peter – Chapter Four

I'm Arming Myself – 1 Peter 4:1-2

Therefore, since Christ suffered in his body, arm yourselves also with the same attitude, because he who has suffered in his body is done with sin. As a result, he does not live the rest of his earthly life for evil human desires, but rather for the will of God. (NIV®)

Just about the whole book of 1 Peter is about suffering as a Christian. So far, most of it has been about how to handle the troubles and trials of life when they happen, especially when they are a result of persecution for our faith. This verse addresses suffering in order to eliminate sin.

I'll have to admit this one is hard to figure out since I can't quite come up with any examples where I've had to suffer in order to resist sin. However the same concept is presented in Hebrews. Hebrews 12:4 *In your struggle against sin, you have not yet resisted to the point of shedding your blood.* (NIV®) In context, the writer to the Hebrews had just explained how many people in the past, from Abel through the prophets and beyond had to give up something to accomplish God's will. Many were killed for their unwillingness to succumb to the demands of others. Prophets, for example, were killed when they refused to stop preaching that Jerusalem would be destroyed for Judah's sins.

You can see why I don't relate to this. But in my own life, I decided that drinking was not something I would do because the spirits in even one beer quenched the Holy Spirit in me enough to make comments that hurt others. Have I suffered because of this? No. Some people may think I'm weird or legalistic, but for me, it has been a good decision. Has it completely eliminated my ability to hurt others by my speech? No, but it has reduced the frequency.

There are many parts of the world where the biggest sin of all, denying Jesus, does bring about bloodshed. I just heard on the news that a mega church in China has been forcibly closed and the pastors told to stop their illegal religious activities. Other churches along with the homes of Christians have been razed by bulldozers. Many were sent to the hospital during that incident.

The Living Bible paraphrases the verses, which sometimes helps and sometimes hinders. It says that I must be ready to suffer. The implication is that I may not have had to suffer physically as a result of sin or in attempting to resist sin. The NIV® and NASB say I'm to arm myself with the attitude of Christ, who suffered. So my conclusion is that while I may not have suffered while resisting sin, I can certainly make up my mind that I will not let physical discomfort prevent me from resisting sin.

How do I arm myself with the attitude that I'll be ready to suffer? Many verses come to my mind. The first is James 1:2-3 *Consider it pure joy, my brothers, whenever you face trials of many kinds, because you know that the testing of your faith develops perseverance.* (NIV®) I have to have a mindset that all trials are there to help me persevere; persevere in the face of sin or persecution or whatever. Hebrews 12:7 *It is for discipline that you have to endure. God is treating you as sons; for what son is there whom his father does not discipline?* (RSV) Hebrews 12:10 *Our fathers disciplined us for a little while as they thought best; but God disciplines us for our good, that we may share in his holiness.* (NIV®) I must look at suffering of any kind as a way that God disciplines me. This is not discipline in the sense of being punished but the same kind of discipline that an athlete goes through so his body will respond correctly when called upon. Suffering produces strength to persevere in the tough times and it gives the training to respond correctly during temptation. This is how suffering does away with sin. It is a long process that eventually leads to holiness.

When I allow suffering to work in me, I will be able to overcome sinful habits; I won't spend the rest of my life wondering if I'm missing out on something. Instead, I'll be eager to do what God wants. I would like to say I'm eager to do what He wants, but it seems that most of the time I'm not. Romans 12:2 *Do not conform any longer to the pattern of this world, but be transformed by the renewing of your mind. Then you will be able to test and approve what God's will is — his good, pleasing and perfect will.* (NIV®) It is a two-step operation. First, I need to stop being conformed to the world's ways and ideologies. These are all the things that say I can be satisfied by something less than God Himself. Then the second step is to be renewed so I can determine His will. I still have a long way to go in yielding to the Holy Spirit so I can do that. However, as I look at each trial and each problem as something that is there to teach me rather than just bad stuff happening, I will move forward.

My Paganism – 1 Peter 4:3-6

For you have spent enough time in the past doing what pagans choose to do — living in debauchery, lust, drunkenness, orgies, carousing and detestable idolatry. They think it strange that you do not plunge with them into the same flood of dissipation, and they heap abuse on you. But they will have to give account to him who is ready to judge the living and the dead. For this is the reason the gospel was preached even to those who are now dead, so that they might be judged according to men in regard to the body, but live according to God in regard to the spirit. (NIV®)

I became a Christian when I was about 28 years old. I had rejected Christianity and my philosophy was that it was OK to do anything as long as no one got hurt. That is pretty much the philosophy of the world today. The only problem with it is that I can't determine if someone is going to be hurt or not by following my own selfish desires. If I choose to spend all my income on my pleasures and myself, then I am hurting others who are in need. Without any way of determining what is OK other than my own perception of what may hurt others, I also failed to understand what would hurt me.

The human mind is very capable of rationalizing just about anything in order to satisfy perceived needs. That is why, after abundant information about the dangers of smoking, people still smoke – even physicians. That is why a person with several DUIs will still drink and drive. That is why the man or woman in a loving marriage will stray and commit adultery. I don't need to list the things I did before I came to Christ or even the sins committed afterward. All I need to do is re-read verse 4 and know I spent way too much time doing those things.

What I do need to do is substitute that attitude of self-indulgence with something else. That is impossible without coming to Christ and having a new birth. Titus 2:11-12 *For the grace of God has appeared for the salvation of all men, training us to renounce irreligion and worldly passions, and to live sober, upright, and godly lives in this world.* (RSV) His grace trains me to live a new life. Without His leading by His Holy Spirit through the Bible, I would have no point of reference regarding what is right or wrong. I would not be able to know what hurts others or myself. More importantly, I would not know what hurts God. With His grace, I am able to know His will and to do things which will please Him. When I do these things, I will not hurt others out of my own sinful self-interest.

Will I be able to avoid hurting other completely? No. However this is my aim: Romans 12:18 *If possible, so far as it depends upon you, live peaceably with all.* (RSV) According to 1 Peter, I won't be able to do that, especially when others heap abuse on me and everyone else who wants to live a godly life. However, I will be able to stand and declare as Paul did in Acts 24:16 *So I always take pains to have a clear conscience toward God and toward men.* (RSV)

One way of doing this is to remember it isn't my job to convict the world of sin and to clean it up. My job is to share the good news of Jesus Christ and do it with words if necessary. My life should reflect my belief and my life should match up with what I say.

I need to warn those who are still caught in the ways of the world. They don't realize that they will have to give an account to Jesus who will judge them. They are currently dead in their sins. (How intolerant of me for saying that.) They will be judged and unless they respond to the Gospel of Jesus Christ, repent of their sins, and turn their lives over to Jesus, they will end up in hell. (Oops, another intolerant attitude.) If they respond then their spirits will be made alive and they will demonstrate it by no longer living the way they are now or the way I did. I will know that I have done the right thing.

The End – 1 Peter 4:7

The end of all things is at hand; therefore, be of sound judgment and sober spirit for the purpose of prayer. (NASB)

My faith is wrapped up in the fact that the end of all things is near. Jesus said I should have an attitude that He could come back at any time. Matthew 24:36-42 is part of His description of the way it will be before the end. The first thing He told us in these verses is that no one knows when the end will come. I vaguely remember someone predicted the end to be some day in 1988. When I first heard it, my thought was that surely Jesus will not return on that day because this guy made the prediction. Currently, everyone is saying the end will be in 2012 because the Mayan calendar runs out then. All this speculation is hogwash because Jesus made it clear no one would know the day or hour, not even the angels in heaven. However, that doesn't mean the end isn't near. Jesus said in these verses that things will appear quite normal before the end. People will be eating, drinking, marrying, and working in the fields. Business will be going on as usual. No one will suspect that in a few minutes, the end will come.

Yes, many have believed that the end is near ever since Jesus left. Peter said it, Paul said it, and the writer to the Hebrews said it. Each one of them tells me how to live in view of that day. The next few verses in 1 Peter are related to how I should live in expectation that Jesus could appear in the next few minutes.

The first priority on this list is prayer. The NIV® says that I should be *clear minded and self-controlled* so that I can pray. The Greek is really fun: *sophroneo* (so-fron-eh'-o); to be of sound mind, i.e. sane, (figuratively) moderate. I need to be sane when it comes to thinking about the end of the world. This would definitely rule out standing on the street corner, dressed in a robe, sporting a long beard and hair, and holding a sign. Crazy people simply do not influence those who need to be warned the end could come at any time.

The next Greek word is: *nepho* (nay'-fo); of uncertain affinity: to abstain from wine (keep sober), i.e. (figuratively) be discreet. I like that last definition. Be discreet. That means to be tactful, cautious, diplomatic, or judicious. I guess I can't just run up to everyone on the street and tell they will go to hell if they don't straighten up before Jesus comes back. While it may be true, it certainly isn't very discreet and therefore probably not very effective.

I don't want to lose the point of being clear minded and self-controlled. It is so I can pray. Jesus also gave a big long list of things that would occur just before He comes back. These are listed in a couple of places but Matthew 24:4-35 is a good one. All sorts of terrible things will happen. Among them will be increased persecution of Christians. This is something that is occurring all around the world. Wickedness will increase. This is also happening but those who are involved don't see it because they have this attitude: Romans 1:32 *Although they know God's righteous decree that those who do such things deserve death, they not only continue to do these very things but also approve of those who practice them.* (NIV®) When all this is happening, Peter warns me not to lose my head, but to know how to pray.

In the middle of Jesus' description of pending events, He says: Matthew 24:20-21 *Pray that your flight will not take place in winter or on the Sabbath. For then there will be great distress, unequaled from the beginning of the world until now — and never to be equaled again.* (NIV®) I believe one thing I should do is pray for those who are persecuted. Pray for their escape and their needs. Prayer has a way of leading to action. That is one reason I'm involved with Serving Others Worldwide[5] and Vertical World Solutions[6] to help Christians in Pakistan. Christians are experiencing persecution and are kept in economic slavery as well. They are in constant need of food, clothing, and Bibles. They need prayer to keep their faith in the midst of very trying times.

I can also pray for myself and those around me so we will be able to stand strong should trials befall us. I would also pray as Paul asked: Colossians 4:3 *And pray for us, too, that God may open a door for our message, so that we may proclaim the mystery of Christ, for which I am in chains.* (NIV®) Paul knew firsthand about trials, yet was always looking for a way to proclaim the Christian faith in the middle of them.

Above All – 1 Peter 4:8

Above all hold unfailing your love for one another, since love covers a multitude of sins. (RSV)

There are a few "above all" commands in the Bible. Of course, different versions phrase it a bit differently but here are some of them.

1 Chronicles 16:25 *For great is the Lord and most worthy of praise; he is to be feared above all gods.* (NIV®) The first "above all" I found is the command to fear the Lord above all other gods. This is also recorded as a psalm of David. He wrote this when he brought the ark of God into Jerusalem. In the psalm, he recounts a brief history of God's miracles, His provision, and His character. He compares God

---

[5] http://www.servingothers.org/Pakistan.html
[6] http://verticalworldsolutions.com/

with the idols in other nations. He also wrote in 1 Chronicles 16:34 *Give thanks to the Lord, for he is good; his love endures forever.* (NIV®) While I need to have the proper respect (fear) for God, this psalm also reminds me that all of my sins are covered because of His great love. The fear comes because I know I don't deserve His love. There is nothing I can do to earn it. He loves me because of His nature and because He sent Jesus to pay for my sins. I can know Him because I accept Jesus. However, can you imagine what it would be like for someone to spurn God's love by rejecting Jesus and what He went through to cover sin? That person should have a fear of God, but it would be a fear of judgment. 1 Chronicles 16:33 *for he comes to judge the earth.* (NIV®)

Proverbs 4:23 *Above all else, guard your heart, for it is the wellspring of life.* (NIV®) It is important for me to guard my heart. It isn't just the physical organ which pumps my blood, but represents my soul. Jesus put it this way: Matthew 15:18-19 *But what comes out of the mouth proceeds from the heart, and this defiles a man. For out of the heart come evil thoughts, murder, adultery, fornication, theft, false witness, slander.* (RSV) The Bible says the heart is deceitful (Jeremiah 17:9). It also says God will give me a new heart. Ezekiel 11:19 *I will give them an undivided heart and put a new spirit in them; I will remove from them their heart of stone and give them a heart of flesh.* (NIV®) I get a new heart when Jesus takes up residence there by faith (Ephesians 3:17). Because Jesus is there, I need to guard what I take into my soul. I don't want to dump garbage on my Lord. I don't want to expose my heart to junk that takes my mind and my thoughts away from His kingdom and His goals. As an example I have to be careful to screen TV commercials as well as shows to make sure I'm not buying into the world's value system. I have to eliminate anything (books, movies, acquaintances) which could lead me into sexual sin, greed, envy, lust, being judgmental, or any other evil that would then come out of my heart and turn into speech and actions.

James 5:12 *But above all, my brethren, do not swear, either by heaven or by earth or with any other oath, but let your yes be yes and your no be no, that you may not fall under condemnation.* (RSV) This is a command to be honest. It is a command to keep promises. I really get sick every time I see some character on TV saying to someone, "I promise I won't let you be hurt." The promise may be different but the situation is clearly out of the person's control. There is no way he or she can keep the promise. I think they are sending the wrong message to kids and adults alike. The message is that I can promise anything but if the circumstances change, then I don't have to complete it. It sets the stage for a multitude of sins. The command is to be honest in life, whether it is in marriage, business, with friends or children. The implication is that making a promise and breaking it is a sin. There will be condemnation, if not consequences. Love isn't going to break those promises, thereby covering over, or better yet, avoiding sins.

2 Peter 1:20-21 *Above all, you must understand that no prophecy of Scripture came about by the prophet's own interpretation. For prophecy never had its origin in the will of man, but men spoke from God as they were carried along by the Holy Spirit.* (NIV®) I think this could be the root of all the other "above all" commands. This is the very basis for my faith; the Bible is the very words of God spoken through men. If I don't have this as a firm foundation, then none of the other commands in the Bible are worth anything. If the Bible isn't the words of God, then they have no authority. They may be very nice principles to live by, but they are optional. Because these words come from God, I can compare any other writing to them to determine if the other is truth or lie. If the Bible says there is only one way to the Father and that is through Jesus, and another "scripture" says that there are many ways, I know the latter is lying. If another "scripture" says that I need Jesus and works, Jesus and someone else, or Jesus and anything else, then I know it is also lying. This is why I must know what the Bible says. Otherwise I can be swayed by any teacher or charlatan who comes to town. Even worse, if I don't know the Bible, then I can be swayed by my own evil desires. When I obey this "above all" I will know Jesus for who He is, turn to Him for my salvation, repent, and have Him living in my heart by faith. The multitude of my sins will be forgiven. My life may not become perfect but it will be better and multitudes of sin will be avoided.

Hospitality – 1 Peter 4:9

Practice hospitality ungrudgingly to one another. (RSV)

I was going to write about my failings in being hospitable but that doesn't seem to be very enlightening. I don't think of myself as having the gift of hospitality but this verse isn't dealing with gifts. The next verse talks about that; this one is a command without reference to a gift. It means I am to practice hospitality whether or not it is a gift. If I think it isn't my gift and use that as an excuse, then I'm just plain being disobedient.

Romans 12:13 *Share with God's people who are in need. Practice hospitality.* (NIV®) One aspect of hospitality is sharing with God's people who are in need. This Christmas was a great time of sharing with others who were in need. Our Bible study group was able to share with families in our church and also with families in Pakistan. It doesn't take much effort to find someone in need. Galatians 6:10 says to do good to all people. Our hospitality shouldn't be limited to other believers, but we should be especially attentive to other believers.

Hebrews 13:2 *Do not neglect to show hospitality to strangers, for thereby some have entertained angels unawares.* (RSV) 3 John 5-8 *Dear friend, you are faithful in what you are doing for the brothers, even though they are strangers to you. They have told the church about your love. You will do well to send them on their way in a manner worthy of God. It was for the sake of the Name that they went out, receiving no help from the pagans. We ought therefore to show hospitality to such men so that we may work together for the truth.* (NIV®) In the U.S. we don't see traveling evangelists and others who spread the gospel without first raising support. It was common in the first century for people to welcome itinerate preachers. They would offer them food and shelter for as long as they were in town. The book of Acts is full of Paul's journeys where others welcomed him and provided for his needs. On occasions, he had to work because there wasn't anyone to provide.

We occasionally have missionaries visit our Bible study group. We always try to take up a collection for them. While the collection doesn't offer a lot in their overall needs, it usually covers their expenses for coming, for babysitters for their children, as well as a little left over.

While I don't feel like I have a gift of hospitality, I do like to share with God's people who are in need as well as with the brothers and sisters who are sharing the gospel.

Using God's Gifts 1 Peter 4:10-11

As each one has received a special gift, employ it in serving one another, as good stewards of the manifold grace of God. Whoever speaks, let him speak, as it were, the utterances of God; whoever serves, let him do so as by the strength which God supplies; so that in all things God may be glorified through Jesus Christ, to whom belongs the glory and dominion forever and ever. Amen. (NASB)

God has given me a gift. The NIV® says "whatever gift." The first thing I think about is the various gifts that are mentioned in the Bible. In Matthew 25:14-15 Jesus tells a parable about a man who gave monetary gifts to three servants. Each received a different amount. By comparison, the first received five times the last. The same applies to the gifts of the Holy Spirit. No one receives the exact same gifts. Just as each person's DNA is different from every other person, the Holy Spirit has given me gifts that are different from every other person's. Romans 12:6 *We have different gifts, according to the grace given us. If a man's gift is prophesying, let him use it in proportion to his faith.* (NIV®)

I think it is a big mistake for anyone to believe a motivational speaker who claims we can do great things just as Moses did, if we let God use us. It was clear in the O.T. that God chose Moses to do a specific job. Some of the Israelites must have heard the same motivational you-can-do-anything speaker and decided they could also lead Israel. In Numbers 16 the story is told how Korah and 250 men decided they had the same gifts as Moses and Aaron. The scary part is that they really thought God had gifted them the same as Moses. God killed them all. The only thing that can come of this kind of you-can-do-anything reasoning is jealousy, guilt over failure, and/or a destroyed ministry.

Attitude is everything. Since I know I have a gift, the verse says I should use it to serve others as a good steward of that gift. Instead of wondering what great things I can do in Jesus' name, I should be concerned about serving others. If God is going to make the gift into a ministry that saves millions or He makes it into a ministry that cleans the kitchen, both are pleasing to God. The parable of the gifts reveals the heart of God. In Matthew 25:16-30 the story is completed when the Master returns and rewards the two servants for using their gifts but punishes the one who didn't use his. The rewards were the same for the two, even though their gifts and results were different.

The importance of using the gifts is emphasized in 1 Peter 4:11. The astounding statement is made that a person gifted with speaking should do it as if God is speaking through him. With crazy people claiming to speak for God, as well as nationally known evangelists, how can I take this verse seriously? It can only be done through humility. When I become proud in doing God's work, using God's gift, God is no longer in it. Sure, some good things can still happen in my ministry, but good things can happen in a totally secular ministry as well.

Whether speaking or serving, the incredible knowledge that it is God doing the work and not me should keep me from becoming proud or thinking I should be doing something greater than He has ordained. I should be depending 100% on His strength to complete the work, whether it is speaking to millions or one person, cleaning a toilet bowl or painting a majestic mural of the Last Supper. It also takes prayer, a good grasp of God's Word, and other godly people to discern where He is leading.

God's grace is manifold, which means having many forms or applications. He knows what He is doing and has orchestrated this world and the gifts given to people in it to accomplish His will. I am to participate willingly with the correct attitude, not trying on my own to do more or less than what He wants. When that happens, I'll be doing it for the glory of God through Jesus.

More Testing – 1 Peter 4:12-13

Beloved, do not be surprised at the fiery ordeal among you, which comes upon you for your testing, as though some strange thing were happening to you; but to the degree that you share the sufferings of Christ, keep on rejoicing; so that also at the revelation of His glory, you may rejoice with exultation. (NASB)

I wonder how many people come to Christ and think He is going to solve all their problems. They may have heard the Gospel message of forgiveness and peace with God. In some cultures, this would be equated with prosperity and good health. After all, don't many pagans sacrifice or pray to gods so that they will be blessed by these gods?

Even among Christian churches, the message is preached that if we do what God wants and have faith, He will do whatever we ask.

This passage in Peter isn't the first time and it isn't the last that suffering as a part of a normal Christian life has been presented. It is in complete agreement with what Jesus taught. Since this has been discussed in previous sections, I won't go over all that again.

A key in this passage is that I shouldn't be surprised when a fiery ordeal happens. If I'm surprised, then I must not have been reading the Bible and understanding what Jesus taught. I may have been listening to someone who I thought was a good preacher but who has his own agenda instead of God's. I can only be surprised if I'm not anticipating problems and if I haven't prepared myself to stand firm in the face of temptations. This is a call to be prepared to battle life's problems from a spiritual standpoint.

Another key is that the ordeals are fiery. In the Greek, fiery trial or fiery ordeal is one word, *purosis* (poo'-ro-sis); ignition, i.e. (specifically) smelting (figuratively, conflagration, calamity as a test). Smelting takes very intense heat. A conflagration is a large fire which causes a great deal of damage. Peter wasn't talking about stubbing my toe; he was talking about some extreme difficulties in life. These are earth-shattering events which would cause most people to rethink their priorities and what is most important.

If I had just come to Christ and then something like this happened, would I wonder if I had made the wrong decision? I've seen it happen to others. They think they have either signed up on the wrong side and go back to their former religion or that God isn't who they thought so they abandoned their newfound faith. I clearly remember a co-worker who only turned to Jesus as a test to see if things would get better for him. When his problems weren't solved, he renounced his decision to follow Christ. Unfortunately for him, things continued in a downward spiral. I remember a person who renounced his previous faith at his baptism, yet several years later turned back to it.

Jesus' parable clearly fits these reactions to trials. Matthew 13:20-21 *The one who received the seed that fell on rocky places is the man who hears the word and at once receives it with joy. But since he has no root, he lasts only a short time. When trouble or persecution comes because of the word, he quickly falls away.* (NIV®) Peter also addresses this in 2 Peter 2:20-22 *For if, after they have escaped the defilements of the world through the knowledge of our Lord and*

Savior Jesus Christ, they are again entangled in them and overpowered, the last state has become worse for them than the first. For it would have been better for them never to have known the way of righteousness than after knowing it to turn back from the holy commandment delivered to them. It has happened to them according to the true proverb, The dog turns back to his own vomit, and the sow is washed only to wallow in the mire. (RSV)

Earlier, Peter explained that trials are there to prove the genuineness of our faith (1 Peter 1:7). My co-worker's faith was proved to be false. I'm not speculating about this; I asked him point blank why he turned away and reverted to his old ways. He admitted that he was only testing Jesus to see if it would benefit him. This man had the knowledge of Jesus but didn't want to submit to Him. It was a "me" decision, not a decision to follow Jesus.

The sad part is that when Jesus is revealed, my co-worker and any others who have failed the fiery tests will not be overjoyed. They will not be able to look forward to an eternity when the trials will be over. They will only look forward to eternal fiery trials because their faith was not genuine in the beginning. If their faith had been genuine, they would not have departed. Peter will address this in 1 Peter 5:10.

The expectation of eternal rejoicing with Jesus is a blessing that kept the Christians of the first few centuries going through their persecution. How much more, as we draw closer to the return of Christ, should we remain steadfast in the face of all kinds of trials and temptations?

Suffering Because There Is Only One Way – 1 Peter 4:14-16

If you are reviled for the name of Christ, you are blessed, because the Spirit of glory and of God rests upon you. By no means let any of you suffer as a murderer, or thief, or evildoer, or a troublesome meddler; but if anyone suffers as a Christian, let him not feel ashamed, but in that name let him glorify God. (NASB)

It's hard to break these passages about suffering and persecution into small chunks because they all build on one another. Previously, Peter talked about fiery trials and now he is talking about being reviled or insulted. There seems to be a big difference between a fiery trial and someone insulting me. However, as any child knows, the constant verbal abuse hurts longer than a physical blow.

Why would someone insult me because of the name of Christ? What is there about Jesus that causes people to insult His followers?

The first thing is that Jesus made the very clear statement He is the only way to God. John 14:6-7 *Jesus answered, "I am the way and the truth and the life. No one comes to the Father except through me. If you really knew me, you would know my Father as well. From now on, you do know him and have seen him."* (NIV®) If a person belongs to a different faith, then my claim to follow Jesus is a statement that he will not go to heaven when he dies. The second thing is Jesus' statement declares that he doesn't really know God. My faith is a statement that unless he renounces his faith and turns to Jesus, he will end up in hell. That is a very heavy thing to lay on a person who may have spent his whole life following a creed that either said his was the only way to God or that there were many ways. Even if his faith is to say there is no God, I have stated he is wrong, dead wrong. His response will be essentially the same as a child who has been insulted. He will respond with an insult or worse.

Understanding the message of Jesus and the cross actually insults others helps me to accept the returned insults. How should I respond when others are offended by the Gospel? Look at Jesus' response. Matthew 15:12-14 *Then the disciples came and said to him, "Do you know that the Pharisees were offended when they heard this saying?" He answered, "Every plant which my heavenly Father has not planted will be rooted up. Let them alone; they are blind guides. And if a blind man leads a blind man, both will fall into a pit."* (RSV) Jesus' response is just as difficult to accept as the fact that only His followers will see God. He recognized those who were offended by His message were not God's children. He said to let them go. Ignore their insults. They are responding to the spirit which they follow (Satan). I need to expect they will insult me and not be surprised, and therefore not take it personally. In fact, I should have a sense of sorrow for them. They are leading each other into a pit which is an eternal one.

Did I get Jesus' message wrong? Was He really as intolerant as it appears? Paul's understanding expands on the message of the cross in 1 Corinthians 1:18-29. In this passage Paul affirms several things about Jesus' message of salvation.

- To the blind, the ones who are perishing, the message is foolishness
- To the ones who are being saved, it is God's power
- God will destroy and frustrate man's wisdom which is contrary to the cross
- Man's wisdom (wisdom that doesn't agree with Jesus) is foolishness
- It was God's wisdom to make sure these can't know Him by their own "wisdom"
  - Wise men
  - Scholars
  - Philosophers
- Those who believe Jesus will be saved even though it seems foolish
- Jesus is a stumbling block to Jews
- Jesus is foolishness to Gentiles
- Jesus is salvation for both Jews and Gentiles who accept that
  - God's foolishness is wiser than man's wisdom
  - God's weakness is stronger than man's strength
- God did this so that no one can boast before Him

That last point is important. Jesus takes away all the boasting about how good I am or that I have somehow earned the right to heaven, whether it is through endless reincarnations or living a good life. Only dependence upon Jesus' gift of eternal life can get me into heaven. Only by knowing Jesus can I know God.

Back to suffering; it seems Peter is telling me that if I'm suffering, I might as well have a good reason for it and therefore steal or make trouble for others. He clearly says that it is not a valid reason for suffering. Not being a troublemaker implies that when I'm insulted, I certainly should not retaliate. I need to learn how to let it go and not get into fruitless arguments with those who insult me.

On the other hand, I should not be ashamed to suffer as a Christian. Persecution and suffering generally causes poverty and oppression. It may mean that I am not able to care for my family the way I want. To some, that would be a disgrace. If a person turns to

Christ and his parents then ridicule or disown him; that would be a great embarrassment in some cultures. Parents accepting Christ may embarrass their children and the children may try to use guilt to turn their parents from Jesus. Peter says that even in these circumstances, God's Spirit and His glory rest on us. I need to remember my goal is to please our heavenly Father, even when it may result in embarrassment on earth. This will bring praise to God.

What Happens to Nominal Christians? – 1 Peter 4:17-19

For the time has come for judgment to begin with the household of God; and if it begins with us, what will be the end of those who do not obey the gospel of God? And "If the righteous man is scarcely saved, where will the impious and sinner appear?" Therefore let those who suffer according to God's will do right and entrust their souls to a faithful Creator. (RSV)

When Peter was writing this, Christians were undergoing some of the fiercest persecutions that occurred during the first 300 years after Christ. From Peter's viewpoint, it was God's judgment on the Church, not a judgment of punishment, but a judgment of refining. He started this letter explaining that the trials come so my faith would be proved genuine. Peter could see what the members of Christ's Body were like. He knew some were living a life that was what we would call "nominal." The word means "in name only". Nominal Christians are people who call themselves Christian without having any life commitment to Jesus.

How does this happen? One way is that their parents belonged to a Christian church and so they believe they are also Christians. Another way is they may attend a Christian church on occasion. They may live in a Christian nation – one where the majority faith is Christian – regardless of the fact that few actually are committed to that faith.

What would my faith look like if I were a nominal Christian? I would visit a church on Easter, Christmas or even monthly. In other words, I have no commitment to worship God. After all, Sunday is the only day I have to sleep in. I own one or two Bibles but I haven't read it in recent memory. I believe God is real and that Jesus was somehow connected to Him. I believe the 10 commandments are good but I can't recall more than two. I believe I'm a good person even though

I've broken most of the commandments. In fact, I would see myself as better than most people and therefore I believe I would be near the front of the line to get into heaven. I give very little if anything to my church. I do what I please during the week with little or no regard to how God might want me to live.

Why would God bring judgment on the household of God? If His Church has many nominal Christians among its members, perhaps He wants to wake them up. Ephesians 5:25-27 *Husbands, love your wives, just as Christ loved the church and gave himself up for her to make her holy, cleansing her by the washing with water through the word, and to present her to himself as a radiant church, without stain or wrinkle or any other blemish, but holy and blameless.* (NIV®) Jesus wants His Church to be holy, without stain, wrinkle, or any other blemish. If I look at the members of a church from Jesus' perspective, I would be able to see into the depths of each heart. I would be able to see the nominal Christians, the weak Christians, and the strong. Would any of these be a blemish? Ask those outside the church. They see the hypocrisy. Of course, they don't like the strong Christians either, but that is their perspective.

What does God's judgment of His Church look like? Revelation 2:4-5 *But I have this against you, that you have abandoned the love you had at first. Remember then from what you have fallen, repent and do the works you did at first. If not, I will come to you and remove your lampstand from its place, unless you repent.* (RSV) The church, the group of people meeting at a certain place, will eventually disappear. This is what happened to the church at Ephesus. No traces of that organization can be found. This occurs all over the U.S. when a church abandons the Gospel and starts teaching other doctrines. The congregation dwindles and the doors are eventually closed.

If the church is strong, then it will survive the trials. Revelation 2:10 *Do not fear what you are about to suffer. Behold, the devil is about to throw some of you into prison, that you may be tested, and for ten days you will have tribulation. Be faithful unto death, and I will give you the crown of life.* (RSV) The reference to having ten days of tribulation is not necessarily a promise that the worst I will face is only ten days in prison. It is, however, an indication that any trial is only temporary. See 2 Corinthians 4:16-18 where Paul assures me that my trials on earth are only temporary. Temporary refers only to the things which happen here on earth. Otherwise, I would not be able to accept Jesus' command to be faithful unto death. A strong church is going to know that all persecutions are there for testing, to cleanse the church of those who claim to be followers of Christ or shake them up so they will be committed to Jesus. As Peter said, when I suffer for Christ, I need to do it because I'm entrusting my soul to a faithful Creator.

What about Judgment on those opposed to Christ, who don't accept the Gospel of Jesus? Psalm 1:4-5 *Not so the wicked! They are like chaff that the wind blows away. Therefore the wicked will not stand in the judgment, nor sinners in the assembly of the righteous.* (NIV®) There will be a time when the whole earth is judged. God isn't going to put up with sinful mankind forever. He gives us every chance to repent. 2 Peter 3:9 *The Lord is not slow about his promise as some count slowness, but is forbearing toward you, not wishing that any should perish, but that all should reach repentance.* (RSV) Some think that because God's judgment hasn't happened, it never will. They can't see beyond their own existence and measure everything by what they see. They even deny that any will perish (go to hell). Peter is warning them that when God's judgment starts, it may very well be too late.

John saw a vision of this judgment in Revelation 6:15-17 *Then the kings of the earth and the great men and the generals and the rich and the strong, and every one, slave and free, hid in the caves and among the rocks of the mountains, calling to the mountains and rocks, "Fall on us and hide us from the face of him who is seated on the throne, and from the wrath of the Lamb; for the great day of their wrath has come, and who can stand before it?"* (RSV) These people are afraid of God's judgment. They are trying to hide rather than welcoming an end to sin and evil. They have made their choice to reject Jesus and therefore God. They are now trying to hide. It won't work. They can't hide from Him.

Where will you be when God's judgment falls? Will you be trying to hide under a rock or will you be receiving a crown of life? Jesus paved the way to that crown of life if you are willing to follow Him more than "in name only."

First Peter – Chapter Five

Leadership – 1 Peter 5:1-4

Therefore, I exhort the elders among you, as your fellow elder and witness of the sufferings of Christ, and a partaker also of the glory that is to be revealed, shepherd the flock of God among you, exercising oversight not under compulsion, but voluntarily, according to the will of God; and not for sordid gain, but with eagerness; nor yet as lording it over those allotted to your charge, but proving to be examples to the flock. And when the Chief Shepherd appears, you will receive the unfading crown of glory. (NASB)

It would be easy for most people to overlook this passage because it is directed to elders or leaders in the Church. However, when I look at the Body of Christ, I discover that each of us is an elder in some respect. I may not have an official leadership role, but if I have children, then I should apply this to the way I lead my family. If I've been a Christian for any length of time, there is going to be someone who is watching me and learning from the way I live. There is also the possibility of meeting informally with a couple of others for Bible study, prayer, or encouragement. If so, then this applies.

Peter demonstrates in verse one that there are times when I must raise my voice slightly to be heard above the crowd. He has some important words of encouragement and correction so he gently reminds (exhorts) his readers that his words should be heeded and put into practice. As he exerts his authority, he also is humble by stating that he is an elder among the others. If I want to be a good leader I must know how to exercise authority and at the same time not let that authority make me proud or feel better than others. Peter does it by identifying himself as part of the group.

On the other hand, Peter also lets his readers know that he has been around longer and has seen Jesus suffer. His words are not without experience. Instead of a telling someone to do something just because he says so, Peter gives an example of why he should be heard. However, he didn't go into great detail, as that would have been too much. I need to know when to use personal examples; I must not go overboard, otherwise the listeners will think I'm trying to show off.

Peter's opening comments are like bookends. First comes the support of "I'm one of you," followed by the authority example, then again supported at the end by identifying with his readers as he mentions he also is a partaker of the glory that will be revealed. The implication of this last comment refers back to the glory to be given when Jesus comes back. That glory is preceded by suffering – something Peter knew all about.

Are you in a position of leadership? If you are, what is your attitude about it? Peter knew that many who serve do it because they feel pressured into it. They don't know how to say, "No," when asked and they don't know how to determine if it is God's will that they should be in this leadership role. As a result, they don't serve with joy so will not do a good job of it.

Coming into a position of leadership can happen in various ways. The most common way is when the qualities of leadership are observed and they are asked to become a leader. This is the way God works through leaders to bring about new ones. I've been in this situation and firmly believed I wouldn't have been asked if God hadn't put it on my pastor's heart to ask me to lead our home Bible study group.

Sometimes there are no leaders and someone volunteers to take over. Hopefully, before doing this, he or she would have been praying about it and would have asked the advice of some godly people to confirm it.

This can also be the result of a direct call from God. A good example is Gideon in Judges 6:11 and the following verses. No one was stepping up to lead Israel so God picked the person He wanted. Gideon was reluctant at first but went on to do great things as God worked through him.

In each of these situations, God can accomplish much. However, I should remind myself how I came into that position; otherwise I can end up doing it under compulsion rather than willingly.

It seems that even in Peter's era, there were leaders who looked at their position as a job instead of a calling from God. They were more interested in seeing how much money they could make rather than serving their congregation. I've heard of people going to school to become a pastor simply because they thought it would be a good job. I don't know where they got their guidance. Many pastors have to work a second job to support their families. The pastors I know usually work a lot more than 40 hours a week. The only ones who seem to be doing well financially are on TV and are using questionable theology to get rich. Peter was clear – that should not be the attitude of a Christian leader. Jesus was pretty clear about it, too. Mark 10:42-45 *Jesus called them together and said, "You know that those who are regarded as rulers of the Gentiles lord it over them, and their high officials exercise authority over them. Not so with you. Instead, whoever wants to become great among you must be your servant, and whoever wants to be first must be slave of all. For even the Son of Man did not come to be served, but to serve, and to give his life as a ransom for many."* (NIV®)

This leads right into Peter's conclusion. When Jesus (who exhibited the qualities of selflessness) appears, He will give a crown of glory to the elders who have been leading with the right attitude. Shepherds were servants. They didn't receive any glory for their hard work. They had to give of themselves to care for their sheep. We can enjoy the current rewards of fellowship and seeing people cared for, but even these are temporary. However, like Jesus, we need to look ahead into eternity to see the real rewards of being a leader.

Respect – 1 Peter 5:5-6

Likewise you that are younger be subject to the elders. Clothe yourselves, all of you, with humility toward one another, for "God opposes the proud, but gives grace to the humble." Humble yourselves therefore under the mighty hand of God, that in due time he may exalt you. (RSV)

Peter just addressed the elders in the church and how they should be leaders, willing and eager to serve, examples to their people, not greedy or lording it over their charges. So now Peter turns his attention to the rest of the church body, those who are younger. The word "likewise" here refers back to the way the elders are to serve. This one little word should stop me in my tracks; I can't think I can slack off because I'm not an elder or in a position of leadership.

There are several words in the Bible which require me to look back at the previous passage for context. The more common words are "therefore" and "since." "Likewise" isn't as common and is translated "in the same way" in other versions. It really doesn't matter what the words are, as I should be looking for them in any form. They tell me there is something very important in the previous passage that is worth rereading; if it is worth rereading, it most likely has an application to my life that I need to work on.

Assuming I have reread the first four verses of the chapter, I see I need to copy the behavior of my church leaders. Rather than taking advantage of elders who are eager to serve, I must be subject to them. That subjection should be by inward obedience with an outward visible show of respect.

In the Old Testament it was expressed in God's Law. Leviticus 19:32 "*Rise in the presence of the aged, show respect for the elderly and revere your God. I am the Lord.*" (NIV®) God connected respect for the elders with the same reverence He expected from His people. Cultures may have different ways of showing respect, such as bowing or removing a hat. Unfortunately, with the mix of many cultures in the U.S., it appears we have lost most outward demonstrations of respect for elders.

Specifically in the Church, I need to obey those who have spiritual authority over me. Hebrews 13:17 *Obey your leaders and submit to their authority. They keep watch over you as men who must give an account. Obey them so that their work will be a joy, not a burden, for that would be of no advantage to you. (*NIV®) I need to remember that their job is to help me in my walk with Christ so when I arrive in heaven, I will be able to hear Jesus say to me, "Well done, my good and faithful servant." Of course, this doesn't mean blind obedience. There are many warnings in Scripture that say some will turn from the faith which even includes some elders. That is why it is important to know the Bible and what it says are the marks of a good elder. If I know the Word then I will be able to discern if the elders are following it and preaching it carefully. When they are, I have good reason to submit to them.

However, it doesn't stop with showing respect only for elders. I should also have humility and show respect at all levels. Not only have many lost respect for their elders, but anyone in their presence. With the onset of cell phones and texting, it appears most people are showing no respect for the person they are with as they take unnecessary calls and chat or text with another person. They ignore the physical person in front of them. You can read the advice columns in the newspaper and the complaints are all consistent. "My _____ (fill in the blank with son, daughter, husband, wife, mother, father, friend, sales clerk, buyer, etc.) doesn't respect me enough to carry on a conversation with me. Instead he lets every cell phone call or text message interrupt him." The problems isn't new, it just has a more annoying manifestation. It can also be TV, computer, radio, newspaper or even a book that you feel is more important than a person.

It takes a lot of grace to be humble when confronted by a person who isn't showing the same reciprocal respect. Peter quoted Proverbs 3:34 *He mocks proud mockers but gives grace to the humble.* (NIV®) There is an implication that when I'm disrespectful it is because I'm proud. Am I so full of myself that whatever I want and whatever I do are more important than anyone around me? The cell phone thing must make the person feel important and therefore proud to be in such demand on the phone. But in doing this, he diminishes the worth of the person he is with. The proverb says that God mocks these people. What do you think it is like to have God mock you?

Proverbs 1:26 *I also will laugh at your calamity; I will mock when panic strikes you.* (RSV) It's pretty clear. Proud people eventually end up paying for their pride. It may be in this life or the next. The last person I want laughing at me in a disaster is God. He is the one I want helping me and He is more than eager to do that. The second chapter of Proverbs is a list of all the things God will do for those who listen to Him. However, it ends with one verse that starts with a big "but." (But is one of those words that should encourage you to reread the previous passage.) Proverbs 2:22 *but the wicked will be cut off from the land, and the unfaithful will be torn from it.* (NIV®)

When others are disrespectful, I must remain humble. God will exalt me when the time is right. If I continue to be a good example, I will receive my rewards from Him. Reread Proverbs 2 and you will see what it means to have God exalt you. He has much in store for us. It all hinges on verse 6. Proverbs 2:6 *For the Lord gives wisdom, and from his mouth come knowledge and understanding.* (NIV®) Wisdom tells me to be humble towards others and under God's mighty hand.

Worry – 1 Peter 5:7

Cast all your anxieties on him, for he cares about you. (RSV)

There are three points in this passage that need clarification: what is anxiety, does God care for me, and how do I cast my anxieties. The first thing to consider is what makes up anxieties. According to the Encarta Dictionary[7], anxieties come in four flavors.

1. Feeling of worry: nervousness or agitation, often about something that is going to happen.
2. Something that worries somebody: a subject or concern that causes worry.
3. Strong wish do to something: the strong wish to do something, especially if the wish is unnecessarily or unhealthily strong
4. Extreme apprehension: psychiatry – a medical condition marked by intense apprehension or fear of real or imagined danger.

The common denominator of 1, 3, and 4 is that the subject of concern has not happened. Only the second definition suggests that the subject of anxiety could have already occurred. While it might make sense to address these differently, the Bible doesn't appear to make a distinction as how to handle the situations.

In Matthew 6:19-34 Jesus addresses the subject of worry and the fact that God does care for me. Most people divide this passage into separate parts, the first dealing with money and the second dealing with worry. However, Jesus put a word in the middle that ties them together. The part about worry starts with the word, "Therefore." The biggest cause of worry is an incorrect perspective on money or things. Jesus sets the correct perspective in verses 19-21 by telling me to store up treasures in heaven so that my heart will be there also. He then reminds me I can't serve two masters. Matthew 6:24 *"No one can serve two masters. Either he will hate the one and love the other, or he will be devoted to the one and despise the other. You cannot serve both God and Money."* (NIV®) The first clue to being able to handle anxiety or worry is to make sure I have a heavenly perspective and to know who I'm serving.

---

[7] Encarta® World English Dictionary [North American Edition] © & (P)2009 Microsoft Corporation. All rights reserved. Developed for Microsoft by Bloomsbury Publishing Plc.

Jesus says not to worry about anything. He talks about food and clothes and the fact that God knows I need these basic of life. He tells me my worth is much greater than that of birds and grass, yet he takes care of the needs of even these. He tells me to contemplate the complexity of a flower and consider that it is much greater than the splendor of the best clothes. If God takes care of the things of nature, how much more is He going to take care of me?

Matthew 6:33 *But seek first his kingdom and his righteousness, and all these things will be given to you as well.* (NIV®) Jesus sums up the proper perspective. When Jesus' kingdom and being righteous is more important than anything else, God will take care of me. Does this mean that I will never be hungry or without clothes? No, Jesus also told me I would have troubles in this life, including persecution. As I look back at the beginning of 1 Peter, I remember what the purpose of suffering is, to get my focus back on the eternal and not the temporal. Isn't it interesting how when one little question or doubt pops up I suddenly lose perspective?

So how do I cast my anxieties on the Lord? There are some examples in Scripture of people doing this. 1 Samuel 1:10 *In bitterness of soul Hannah wept much and prayed to the Lord.* (NIV®) The priest, Eli, observed her praying and after talking with her, he encouraged her with a short prayer of his own. Hannah's face was no longer downcast.

1 Samuel 23:15-16 *While David was at Horesh in the Desert of Ziph, he learned that Saul had come out to take his life. And Saul's son Jonathan went to David at Horesh and helped him find strength in God.* (NIV®) Here is another example of a friend who encourages and helps another who is concerned.

Matthew 26:37-38 *And taking with him Peter and the two sons of Zeb'edee, he began to be sorrowful and troubled. Then he said to them, "My soul is very sorrowful, even to death; remain here, and watch with me."* (RSV) Even Jesus knew that friends can help when in distress.

Jesus prayed, Hannah prayed, and David wrote his prayers down in the Psalms. The Psalms are great examples of David pouring out his heart to God. He didn't deny the problems he was facing or his discouragement. Prayers dealing with anything must be honest. God knows my fears and worries, so denying them will only hurt my communication with Him. I have to be honest in my payers; however,

I don't let that honesty overshadow what God can do. I remember I need an eternal perspective and then trust in God. Psalm 56:3-4 *When I am afraid, I will trust in you. In God, whose word I praise, in God I trust; I will not be afraid. What can mortal man do to me?* (NIV®) David always came back to the basics.

God is in control. This life is only preparing me for eternity. I will maintain the proper eternal perspective with His help.

Philippians 4:6-7 *Do not be anxious about anything, but in everything, by prayer and petition, with thanksgiving, present your requests to God. And the peace of God, which transcends all understanding, will guard your hearts and your minds in Christ Jesus.* (NIV®)

The Enemy – 1 Peter 5:8-9

Be self-controlled and alert. Your enemy the devil prowls around like a roaring lion looking for someone to devour. Resist him, standing firm in the faith, because you know that your brothers throughout the world are undergoing the same kind of sufferings. (NIV®)

The enemies of Christians are not other religions or institutions which persecute or introduce teachings that are contrary to Christ. Some people who believe in other religions are easy to spot. They have traditional garb, jewelry or some other distinguishing marks that tell us they don't follow Jesus. When I see them, I shouldn't consider them enemies, even if they are wearing the uniform of a government that persecutes Christians. If I see them as enemies, then I will not be able to reach them for Jesus. Instead, I will be fearful, disrespectful, or angry when I see them. These emotional reactions will prevent me from telling them about Jesus when I have an opportunity.

How can I keep from having negative thoughts when I see these people? The key is found in Ephesians 6:12 *For we are not contending against flesh and blood, but against the principalities, against the powers, against the world rulers of this present darkness, against the spiritual hosts of wickedness in the heavenly places.* (RSV) My enemy is Satan and all the demonic forces under his control. The people who serve him are his victims. They are flesh and blood people who are trapped in his domain. They have been blinded and confused by the lies he has spread as well as by their own sinful responses. 2 Corinthians 3:14-17 *But their minds were made dull, for to this day the same veil remains when the old covenant is read. It has not been removed, because only in Christ is it taken away. Even to this day when Moses is read, a veil covers their hearts. But whenever anyone turns to the Lord, the veil is taken away. Now the Lord is the Spirit, and where the Spirit of the Lord is, there is freedom.* (NIV®) If I view these people as my enemies rather than people who need to be rescued from Satan's dominion, I will not have the opportunity to be an ambassador for Christ so He can open their eyes to the truth. When they come to Christ they will have freedom from Satan's grasp.

It takes a lot of self-control to be able to keep from hiding my faith in the presence of Satan's servants. It takes self-control to keep from falling into the traps Satan has laid in this world. Self-control sounds like something I have to muster up within myself. However, true self-control is not something I can do on our own. 2 Timothy 1:7 *for God did not give us a spirit of timidity but a spirit of power and love and self-control.* (RSV) Self-control is a product of God's Holy Spirit living in me. Depending on the Holy Spirit is the only way to have success overcoming the temptations in this world, whether they are temptations to do wrong or to avoid doing what God wants me to do.

Resisting the devil requires dependence on the power of God in my life. I have had temptations in my life which I thought were beyond my capability to resist. As I struggled with them, I learned that my thoughts were correct. I was incapable of resisting them by myself. It was then I understood these words from Ephesians 1:19-20 *… the immeasurable greatness of his power in us who believe, according to the working of his great might which he accomplished in Christ when he raised him from the dead …* (RSV) The same resurrection power that God used to raise Jesus from the dead is in every believer, including me. That power gives me self-control only when I rely on it. If I think I can exert enough self-control to overcome a temptation then I'm deceiving myself. When I have faced temptations, relied on God's power in me, and asked Him for that power, His Holy Spirit has given me the power to overcome the temptation. I have experienced James 4:7 in my life. *Submit therefore to God. Resist the devil and he will flee from you.* (NASB) I relied on Jesus and His power in me to resist and the temptation disappeared.

The circumstances that led to the temptation were still there but the desire or motivation to succumb were gone.

When I resist Satan by either sharing Jesus with others who may be hostile to Christ or just by doing right, I may face suffering. Peter reminds me that I'm not alone. We have brothers and sisters in Christ all around the world who are undergoing the same kind of problems that I am. This should be an encouragement to persevere. If they are trusting in the power of Jesus in their lives, then I also should be able to persevere.

Eternal Perspective – 1 Peter 5:10-11

And after you have suffered for a little while, the God of all grace, who called you to His eternal glory in Christ, will Himself perfect, confirm, strengthen and establish you. To Him be dominion forever and ever. Amen. (NASB)

Enough with the suffering! How many times in 1 Peter has suffering been mentioned? He referred to our suffering thirteen times. He referred to Christ's suffering six times. Do you think Peter had a message for us regarding suffering? If you are ever confronted by a person who says you lack faith if you are suffering, point them to the book of 1 Peter. Tell them to read it and explain why Peter continued to encourage the first century saints to endure and even consider suffering commendable before God (1 Peter 2:20).

The great thing about this suffering is that it is only for a little while. Peter knew persecution. He had to flee for his life after he was imprisoned in Jerusalem (Acts 12:4-17). Jesus told Peter he would die for his faith (John 21:18-19). Yet in the midst of this, Peter can say that the suffering is only for a little while.

Peter could speak of suffering as being temporary because he had an eternal perspective. He was looking past the events of this world and could see the eternal results. Just as an athlete endures pain and hardship during training so he can compete in his sport, so I need to view the trials of this world as preparation to receive an eternity without suffering. Psalm 16:11 *You have made known to me the path of life; you will fill me with joy in your presence, with eternal pleasures at your right hand.* (NIV®)

Paul put it this way: 2 Corinthians 4:16-18 *Therefore we do not lose heart. Though outwardly we are wasting away, yet inwardly we are being renewed day by day. For our light and momentary troubles are achieving for us an eternal glory that far outweighs them all. So we fix our eyes not on what is seen, but on what is unseen. For what is seen is temporary, but what is unseen is eternal.* (NIV®)

Peter and Paul could focus on the eternal because they knew that God is the God of all grace and that He has called me, and every Christian, to share in the eternal glory of Christ. They knew God is concerned with each individual. God doesn't delegate the job of maturing me to others. He is the one who is making sure that we are being developed into people who will be strong, firm and steadfast. Psalm 139:2-3 *You know when I sit and when I rise; you perceive my thoughts from afar. You discern my going out and my lying down; you are familiar with all my ways.* (NIV®) Yes, He may use others in my life, but it is God who makes sure His plan is accomplished.

The only way to get through the trials is to make sure I understand who God is, as well as the fact He cares for me individually. Peter says all dominion or power belongs to Him. Now, if I doubt God's ability, I will not be confident when trials and sufferings take place. I will worry and fret because I don't really believe God is able to take care of me. I will look at the suffering as either my own lack of faith or God's inability to sustain me. Either removes all hope for the future.

My faith needs to have a proper understanding of God's plan and that understanding is what Peter has hammered into this epistle over and over. I will suffer. You will suffer. That is the Christian way.

I need to understand that God is good and He has my best interests at heart. That means He will not settle for more now if it means less in eternity. He will not settle for an easy life now if that means less glory in eternity. He has the power and dominion over all things and He knows how to use it for eternal good.

Faithful Friends – 1 Peter 5:12-14

With the help of Silas, whom I regard as a faithful brother, I have written to you briefly, encouraging you and testifying that this is the true grace of God. Stand fast in it. She who is in Babylon, chosen together with you, sends you her greetings, and so does my son Mark. Greet one another with a kiss of love. Peace to all of you who are in Christ. (NIV®)

We all need faithful brothers. We need to have people in our lives who will be faithful when we need help or encouragement. Faithful is the key word. I remember a person whom I respected for his knowledge and kindness. I went to him seeking advice about something. In his wisdom he asked me questions about the decision I was working through. However, after some time I realized he was not providing me any help. He was in essence a very polite and kind "yes" man. He was not faithful to help me find the best answer but was simply affirming what I had already thought, right or wrong. I didn't seek his counsel for anything else because I couldn't trust him to tell me the truth if it wasn't something I had already discovered.

Peter knew about faithful brothers and that they sometimes have to confront me when I'm going in the wrong direction. Galatians 2:11 *When Peter came to Antioch, I opposed him to his face, because he was clearly in the wrong.* (NIV®) Paul had to rebuke Peter when he was wrong. I can't imagine walking up to Peter and telling him he is wrong about something. In Galatians 2:14, Paul says that he did this in front of everyone. Now that is a faithful brother! Paul risked being ostracized and maybe even worse.

A faithful brother is more concerned with pleasing God than pleasing people. Galatians 1:10 *Am I now seeking the favor of men, or of God? Or am I trying to please men? If I were still pleasing men, I should not be a servant of Christ.* (RSV) Without an eternal perspective it is easy to fall into the trap of pleasing people instead of God. This admonition for a faithful brother really only comes into play when pleasing people is opposed to pleasing God. After all, we do have the command to look out for others' interests (Philippians 2:4). However, sometimes looking out for someone's interest means I have to tell him the truth, even if it hurts.

There are many more aspects of being a faithful brother. Colossians 4:12-13 *Epaphras, who is one of your number, a bondslave of Jesus Christ, sends you his greetings, always laboring earnestly for you in his prayers, that you may stand perfect and fully assured in all the will of God. For I bear him witness that he has a deep concern for you and for those who are in Laodicea and Hierapolis.* (NASB) Epaphras was a good example of a faithful bother. He was one who prayed for his friends. Note that he had a great concern for them. A casual acquaintance is seldom a faithful brother. This requires getting to know each other.

Peter reminds his readers his purpose is to encourage them in that what he has said is really from God. Remember that the main topic of this letter is to stand faithful in the face of trials. The ability to stand firm is rooted in the message of salvation and eternal hope we have in Jesus. This salvation is the grace that is from God and it helps me stand through any trials.

Peter ends his letter in the same way as many of the other letters in the New Testament, with greetings from people. We do this all the time when talking on the phone to a relative or friend in a distant location. We say, "Say Hi to Sally (or whoever) for me." Who is sending greetings in this letter? The "she in Babylon" sounds like the Church in Babylon. This is the simplest meaning and fits with the context of Mark sending his greetings. I read the preface to Adam Clark's Commentary where he used several pages to come to this conclusion. He cited many historians and others, then finally concluded that the ancient city of Babylon was still in existence when Peter wrote the letter. He also concluded that Peter was most likely there since there were many Jews living there. The significance is we are people and we really like to acknowledge each other and say, "Hi," when we are far away from people we love and care for.

When we are present with our friends and loved ones, we should show that love. Not all cultures greet each other in the same way. At that time, a kiss was very common. Whatever custom our culture has, we should express love to each other.

With Christ, I can have peace. As I was reminded in previous verses, that peace is only available in Christ. For those outside of Christ, there is not peace but only an expectation of condemnation. Romans 5:1 *Therefore, since we are justified by faith, we have peace with God through our Lord Jesus Christ.* (RSV) Those without Christ don't have peace. Hebrews 10:27 *but only a fearful expectation of judgment and of raging fire that will consume the enemies of God.* (NIV®) Where do you stand? In His grace or outside of it? What is your hope in trials? I pray you know Him and His peace.

Second Peter – Chapter One

Knowledge of Him – 2 Peter 1:1-4

Simon Peter, a servant and apostle of Jesus Christ, To those who through the righteousness of our God and Savior Jesus Christ have received a faith as precious as ours: Grace and peace be yours in abundance through the knowledge of God and of Jesus our Lord. His divine power has given us everything we need for life and godliness through our knowledge of him who called us by his own glory and goodness. Through these he has given us his very great and precious promises, so that through them you may participate in the divine nature and escape the corruption in the world caused by evil desires. (NIV®)

Peter identifies himself with both his original name and the name Jesus gave him. Simon represents his human nature along with his fallibility. As Simon, he identifies with the lowly position of servant. Peter represents his spiritual nature along with the power bestowed on him by Jesus through the Holy Spirit. As Peter, he identifies with the exalted position of an apostle of Jesus Christ. The letter of 2 Peter comes to us with both the authority of Jesus through Peter as well as the identification of a fellow alien in this world through Simon.

This letter is different from 1 Peter in that he is addressing it to a broader audience. 1 Peter was addressed to the dispersed Church while this letter is addressed to all believers of all times. While the first letter dealt with living under persecution, this letter is more prophetic, looking to the future when opposition to Christ will come from within the church as false prophets and then beyond to the last days when philosophers will bring precepts into the world which deny biblical faith. How do I live and conduct myself in these circumstances?

The first thing he reminds me of is that my faith is the same as his. It is just as precious and sincere as the faith he has. The servant and apostle had to come to Jesus by faith just like everyone else. Because Jesus is God and Savior, it is by His righteousness that I have faith. The Gospel never changes. Jesus is righteous, always has been, and always will be. Because He is righteous, when He died on the cross, He could bear my sins (and everyone's) and then give me His righteousness when I turned to Him in faith for the forgiveness of my sins. Amazing how much can be packed into one small verse.

Because I know God and Jesus, I have grace and peace, which comes in abundance. Do you have grace and peace in abundance today? If not, what is keeping it away from you? Peter clearly says it comes through our knowledge of Jesus. I hope I'm not being too simplistic; however, it seems that if I don't have peace and grace, then something is wrong with my knowledge of Jesus. Am I limiting His power in my life because of my lack of knowledge about His power? Am I continuing in some sin because I don't really know what it costs to be forgiven? Have I lost hope and am in despair because I have forgotten what the eternal future holds? All are the results of forgetting or not knowing Jesus as He wants me to know Him.

Peter wants me to know God's divine power is sufficient for anything that faces me in life: all of the problem, heartache, illness, relational problems, and ultimately – death. His power is all I need to live a godly life. There is no need to compromise in this world when I have His power in me. Ephesians 3:20-21 *Now to him who by the power at work within us is able to do far more abundantly than all that we ask or think, to him be glory in the church and in Christ Jesus to all generations, for ever and ever. Amen.* (RSV) When I call upon His power to live a godly life, the glory goes to Jesus, not me. That power enables me to do much more than I ever thought I could. I can resist sin, go longer, and work harder. I can accomplish things I never expected when I let Him work in me.

Peter said His power gives me everything I need for life and godliness. He didn't leave anything out. Try to think of something that His power can't handle. Did you think of something? You're wrong if you did. God doesn't lie and His word isn't wrong. This is one of those very great and precious promises He has given each of us. There is a catch though. It is my knowledge of Him. He gives me all this through my knowledge of Him. It is very easy to fall short by listening to false prophets or the world. They will tell you all sorts of things about God which will keep you from having peace and grace in abundance. Some will promise these very same things but it will be based on works and not His divine power. They may even teach that faith will give you peace and grace, but the faith they teach is faith in their own teaching, not in a true knowledge of God.

Here are some good tests to determine whether or not I'm participating in the divine nature of God. Is my life holy? How is my anger? What is going on in my thought life? Are any of these or other things inconsistent with God's divine nature? If so, then something is wrong and I'm not participating in His nature, but fighting against it. It comes back to a faulty knowledge of God. With His divine nature, there is escape from the corruption in the world. It isn't just suppressing my evil desires, but an escape from them.

I've heard people say it is just their nature to worry. Others also use this excuse for other things, "it's just my nature." But this is not what God intends. If I have been born again my nature is now God's nature. I need to exercise that nature by putting off what I used to do and think and putting on His nature by doing and thinking His way. Then I can say it isn't our nature to worry, or do whatever it was I used to do.

I was going to quote some verses from Romans 8:1-11 to emphasize this new nature, but I would have to quote too much. So please look it up. Let's set our minds on the Spirit and realize in our lives the power of God to overcome the corruption in the world caused by evil desires.

Growing – 2 Peter 1:5-9

For this very reason, make every effort to add to your faith goodness; and to goodness, knowledge; and to knowledge, self-control; and to self-control, perseverance; and to perseverance, godliness; and to godliness, brotherly kindness; and to brotherly kindness, love. For if you possess these qualities in increasing measure, they will keep you from being ineffective and unproductive in your knowledge of our Lord Jesus Christ. But if anyone does not have them, he is nearsighted and blind, and has forgotten that he has been cleansed from his past sins. (NIV®)

Because of His divine power, His great and precious promises, our participation in His nature, and therefore, our ability to escape corruption in the world, God expects something from me. He wants me to exert some effort. Reflect on what He has given us and then consider whether or not some effort on our part is appropriate. Anyone who thinks that living a Christian life should be easy has been fed some misinformation. It does take effort and it isn't always easy. However, I'm not doing it alone. If I try to do it alone it will be impossible. I need to remember that He gives me everything I need to live a victorious Christian life. Even in this, I must depend on Him.

Notice the verse says I need to add to my faith. Faith is the starting point. Faith doesn't come from me; it is the gift of God (Ephesians 2:8). I need to take what God has given me and work with it.

The first thing I'm told to work on is goodness. Before I came to Christ for salvation, I was corrupt as described in Ephesians 4:19. *Having lost all sensitivity, they have given themselves over to sensuality so as to indulge in every kind of impurity, with a continual lust for more.* (NIV®) The world's proverb, "Do unto others before they do it unto you." is a good description of what lies below the surface of every human being. This self-centeredness results in badness instead of goodness.

Becoming good requires a realistic view of what I was and what I should be. Ephesians 4:22-24 *You were taught, with regard to your former way of life, to put off your old self, which is being corrupted by its deceitful desires; to be made new in the attitude of your minds; and to put on the new self, created to be like God in true righteousness and holiness.* (NIV®) This "put off" and "put on" is where the effort comes in. This verse starts with, "You were taught." Think about it. How can a Christian become good if he's been taught all his life that his immoral behavior is normal? Yes, Jesus does clean me up by giving me His Holy Spirit, however I need to pay attention to Scripture so I can discern what is right and wrong. I need to be taught. Learning requires effort and I shouldn't assume that I'll suddenly have the wisdom to know what to do in every circumstance. I need to add to the goodness that I practice more and more knowledge so the goodness will increase and I can move on to the next step.

Self-control seems out of step with what some believe is the way the Holy Spirit works in us. They believe that once you are filled with the Holy Spirit, He will control you and you don't have to work on it. 2 Timothy 1:7 *for God did not give us a spirit of timidity but a spirit of power and love and self-control.* (RSV) It works both ways. His Spirit gives me the willingness and ability to control myself. Without His Spirit, I wouldn't have a desire to be self-controlled in a godly way. The knowledge I received in the previous step points out where I need that self-control. All of these steps are circular in nature. They are like a chain where each link depends on the previous and adds to the next.

How is it possible to persevere without self-control? The world is clamoring for us to go opposite the way of Christ. Every place we go there are enticements to sin. Go to the store and there are things there that I want but can't afford. I sin when I covet those things. Something goes wrong and I'm tempted to complain or grumble. Get on the Internet and it's just me and my imagination so I can indulge in a host of sins from gambling to pornography. Persevering is saying no to all these temptations. The longer I say no, the easier it gets. The temptations don't go away so perseverance must continue.

Perseverance finally leads to godliness. This is a life significantly free from sin. Perseverance in saying no leads to a life that others will recognize as blameless. Looking back at the beginning of the Christian walk, goodness seemed like a huge step. Now, looking from the perspective of godliness, it was just a baby step. It was a step of faith. Now, goodness is almost second nature. (Don't get me wrong, I'm not saying that I or anyone else will ever be free from in sin in this world.)

All of the above has been God-oriented obedience and growth. He doesn't want me to stop there. He wants me to continue to put it into practice so it helps others. True brotherly kindness happens after getting my relationship with God right. It is treating others the way God wants. It is true friendship or brotherly love. It is the spiritual progression from being godly.

Brotherly kindness runs right into love, the kind of love that Jesus has for us. 1 Peter 1:22-23 *Now that you have purified yourselves by obeying the truth so that you have sincere love for your brothers, love one another deeply, from the heart. For you have been born again, not of perishable seed, but of imperishable, through the living and enduring word of God.* (NIV®) I've been born again (came to Jesus in faith) and then purified myself by obeying the truth (the first steps as described above), which should result in brotherly love. Peter then pushes to the next step, which is godly love. This is the fulfillment of our faith on earth. If I truly have godly love for others, I have achieved the unity He expects me to have.

It would seem that at this point I have achieved my goal. However, the next verse lets me know that I will never completely arrive this side of heaven. These qualities are to increase. I need to start back at the top and increase every area listed. Peter knew that we would never be completely loving or godly or self-controlled or anything else. The Christian life is an ongoing progression to become more like Jesus.

When I'm increasing in these qualities, whether I have taken only the first step toward goodness or whether I have advanced and then gone back to improve on any of the qualities, I will be effective and productive in my knowledge of Jesus. Do you feel you are not effective or productive in your Christian walk? Then go back and look for the weak link in the chain. Work on it. Peter said to make every effort. Don't give up.

Do you call yourself a Christian but can't identify with any of these qualities? Peter says that you are nearsighted and blind. Do you know you have been cleansed from your sins? Have you forgotten that? Is it possible that you have not been cleansed from your sins and that is the reason you don't have these qualities? If you haven't been cleansed then you have been calling yourself a Christian without the benefit of knowing Christ. Now is the time either to remember you have been cleansed or to ask Jesus to forgive you and accept His cleansing. Then, move from faith to goodness and start on the progressive road of the Christian life.

Election – 2 Peter 1:10

Therefore, brethren, be the more zealous to confirm your call and election, for if you do this you will never fall. (RSV)

When I first read this in other versions, it sounds almost like Peter is telling me that I had to do these things (the list in the previous verses) in order to keep my salvation. However, this version and the original Greek clarify that what I'm supposed to be doing (confirming my call and election) will keep me from falling or stumbling. It doesn't appear to have anything to do with the possibility of losing my salvation.

The RSV is the only version to use the word zealous in my approach to confirming my call and election. Others use the word eager or diligent. I really like zealous. But, what do I need to do to confirm or make sure of my call and election? The question boils down to, how can I be sure that God has saved me?

The answer lies, not with me and what I've done, but with God and who He is. What are His promises regarding salvation? I need to be eager to find out more about Him and how I'm saved in order to confirm in my own mind that He has saved me and that He won't go back on His promise.

A good starting point is what Jesus said. John 3:16 "*For God so loved the world that he gave his one and only Son, that whoever believes in him shall not perish but have eternal life.*" (NIV®) God initiated the whole thing by giving Jesus to us. It is based on His love for us and not on what I can do. I have some work to do, if you want to call it work. That work is to believe in Jesus. John 6:29 *Jesus answered, 'The work of God is this: to believe in the one he has sent.'* (NIV®) Paul clarified that the ability to believe on Jesus isn't even something I can do without God giving me the ability through the faith He has given me (Ephesians 2:8-9). He also makes sure I understand that this believing isn't the same kind of effort in which I can boast.

In fact, Paul goes even further in saying that this gift of faith is something God had planned on giving us long before we were even born. Ephesians 1:4-5 *For he chose us in him before the creation of the world to be holy and blameless in his sight. In love he predestined us to be adopted as his sons through Jesus Christ…* (NIV®) This is mind boggling if you stop to think about it for a while. Somehow, way before time even began, God knew all about me and decided He wanted me to be holy and blameless, even though He also knew I would be a sinner, much less than holy and blameless. He decided He would have to adopt me as His child in order to be able to make me holy and blameless. The only way to do that was to do it through Jesus. Ephesians 2:13 *But now in Christ Jesus you who once were far away have been brought near through the blood of Christ.* (NIV®) Hebrews 13:12 *And so Jesus also suffered outside the city gate to make the people holy through his own blood.* (NIV®)

He had this great plan in place before I existed. How can I possible think I am saved by anything I've done, other than accepting the gift He has provided? How can I possible think I could somehow do something that would cause God to take that gift away? I've run into people who think that after they have been saved they can commit some horrible sin and lose their salvation. What is interesting is that they are usually people who strongly emphasize the gifts of the Holy Spirit and that these gifts can't be revoked. They quote this verse to prove it. Romans 11:29 *for God's gifts and his call are irrevocable.* (NIV®) What a great verse for this study! It's too bad they don't apply the verse to salvation but only to gifts of the Spirit. Not only does it talk about God's gift, but also His call. Once I'm called, that's it. I'm His and there isn't any way of changing that fact. Once I take hold of the gift of faith that leads to salvation, He will never take it away.

You can go on and find may more verses about God and His promises to us about our election and calling. Romans 8:28-39 is loaded with these promises. He called us, foreknew and predestined us, justified us, intercedes for us, nothing can separate us. They all depend on God and who He is. If your knowledge of God is lacking, then get to know Him better to confirm your election and calling. That's something to be zealous about.

Welcome to Heaven – 2 Peter 1:11

Then God will give you a grand entrance into the eternal Kingdom of our Lord and Savior Jesus Christ. (NLT)

Have you ever wondered what it will be like to enter heaven? There have been many songs written about entering heaven. Some focus on seeing loved ones and other saints who have passed on but really yearning to see Jesus. Others consider what we will do when we first see Jesus. Will we fall on our faces, will we shout with praise, will we be scooped up and hugged by Jesus? One song talks of a welcoming committee of people who have been somehow blessed by our ministry, even by things we never even considered as ministry.

What would a grand entrance, rich welcome, abundantly supplied entrance, or gates opened wide be like, as different versions state? When famous people visit a city, they are often given a key to the city, a symbolic gesture that says all the resources of the city are available to them. Is this what Peter is talking about? Am I going to get keys to heaven when I enter? Think about it, only dignitaries, nobles, or famous people get a key to the city, but God is promising us a grand entrance into heaven. We who were once opposed to God and enemies, we who have done nothing to deserve to be in heaven will be welcomed with great fanfare. It boggles my mind.

Am I only speculating about this? What does other Scripture say about this? The first that comes to mind is Matthew 25:21 *"His master replied, 'Well done, good and faithful servant! You have been faithful with a few things; I will put you in charge of many things. Come and share your master's happiness!'"* (NIV®) There are requirements to hearing the Lord Jesus say this to me. I need to be faithful in a few things. God has placed me here for a purpose and I need to be faithful to Him. He doesn't ask much and He gives me His Holy Spirit to make sure I can do the little that He requests. In the eternal perspective, what He has entrusted to me is little, but what He will give me in eternity is much. That is quite amazing. In addition, He says that by taking charge of the things He has in store for me in heaven, I will be sharing in His happiness. This certainly sounds like I'll have a grand entrance.

Colossians 3:3-4 *For you died, and your life is now hidden with Christ in God. When Christ, who is your life, appears, then you also will appear with him in glory.* (NIV®) This is a big clue as to why I will receive a rich entrance into heaven. I can imagine God standing at the gate to heaven. He looks down the road and sees someone coming. Will He open the gate and welcome this person? He will if He recognizes him. If He sees the person is a dignitary, noble, or fantastically deserving person, God will have a parade with throngs cheering and trumpets blowing. When the person gets near, God breaks out the band and everyone rushes to line the street. Who does God see coming? He sees His own Son. He doesn't see our sins or failures. He only sees the righteousness and holiness of Jesus. Yes, He knows that hidden in the image of Jesus is John or Jane Doe. But Jesus died for me and that means He will welcome me just as He would welcome His own Son.

Matthew 16:19 *"I will give you the keys of the kingdom of heaven, and whatever you bind on earth shall be bound in heaven, and whatever you loose on earth shall be loosed in heaven."* (RSV) Jesus has already given me the keys to heaven. I have, through Him, access to everything that heaven has to offer. Jesus is the way to heaven and no one will be able to enter without Him. Not only do I have entrance to Heaven but I can call on Him now to provide what is needed to further His kingdom on earth. John 15:7-8 *"If you remain in me and my words remain in you, ask whatever you wish, and it will be given you. This is to my Father's glory, that you bear much fruit, showing yourselves to be my disciples."* (NIV®) I have the Gospel message which will loose any who respond and will actually bind or condemn any who hear and reject it.

Revelation 3:21 *"To him who overcomes, I will give the right to sit with me on my throne, just as I overcame and sat down with my Father on his throne."* (NIV®) Not only will I be treated as royalty when I enter heaven, but I will become royalty. Don't ask me how this works. I don't know how each person who enters heaven will be able to rule with Jesus. The question is, who will I rule over if everyone is ruling? Beats me, I only know what I read. I also know this: 1 Peter 2:9 *But you are a chosen race, a royal priesthood, a holy nation, God's own people, that you may declare the wonderful deeds of him who called you out of darkness into his marvelous light.* (RSV) This all fits together in heaven.

I certainly don't want to miss out on it. Do you? He has promised us this great entrance, but the greatest part of it will be to see God the Father, Jesus the Son, and the Holy Spirit as they truly are. Revelation 22:17 *The Spirit and the bride say, "Come!" And let him who hears say, "Come!" Whoever is thirsty, let him come; and whoever wishes, let him take the free gift of the water of life.* (NIV®) If you thirst and yearn to see Jesus, to see evil ended, to be done with sin, then the invitation is open to have a grand entrance into heaven.

Reminders – 2 Peter 1:12-15

For this reason I will not be negligent to remind you always of these things, though you know and are established in the present truth. Yes, I think it is right, as long as I am in this tent, to stir you up by reminding you, knowing that shortly I must put off my tent, just as our Lord Jesus Christ showed me. Moreover I will be careful to ensure that you always have a reminder of these things after my decease. (NKJV)

What is it about us that we need reminders even when we already know? Peter certainly knew that after he died people would need some reminders of what he and the other apostles had taught. Peter was moved by the Holy Spirit as he wrote this and it emphasizes what God has done throughout the Bible.

Exodus 13:9-10 *This observance will be for you like a sign on your hand and a reminder on your forehead that the law of the Lord is to be on your lips. For the Lord brought you out of Egypt with his mighty hand.* (NIV®) One of the most notable reminders in the Old Testament is the Passover feast. The whole ceremony recounts how God was faithful to bring the Israelites out of Egypt. It recounts the bitterness of their slavery and the process God used to wear down the Egyptians. The culmination of the feast reminds the Israelites the blood of an innocent lamb was required to protect them from the same fate the Egyptians received – death of the firstborn in each household.

That reminder also foreshadows God's liberating all mankind from slavery to sin. Just as Israel was in bondage to Egypt, every person on the earth is in bondage to sin. Sin results in a bitter life. One that never satisfies but always requires more and more to get the same thrills. Ephesians 4:19 *They don't care anymore about right and wrong and have given themselves over to impure ways. They stop at nothing, being driven by their evil minds and reckless lusts.* (TLB) Of course, the end result is spiritual and physical death.

The lesson of the Passover is that God is at work in all sorts of ways to get my attention and bring me to a point where I will listen to Him. Israel had to endure many of the plagues God brought upon Egypt. In addition, Israel was treated harshly and many times blamed Moses for increasing their bitter bondage. In the same way, many people blame for their problems the messenger who carries the Gospel. They don't like to hear that their own sinful behavior has caused most of the difficulties in their lives.

The climax of the Passover is when the lamb must be sacrificed. Its blood is spread on the lintel (top beam over the door) and doorpost of the house. The lamb is cooked and eaten, but they have to be careful not to break any of its bones. This prophesies the death of the Lamb of God, Jesus. Jesus shed His blood on a cross – a beam and supporting post. None of His bones were broken. When the destroying angel saw the blood of the lamb on the doors of the Israelites, he passed over them. When God judges the world and sees the blood of Jesus applied to the lives of His people, He will pass over our sins and we will not have to pay the penalty for them. God will see Jesus has already done that.

Jesus proclaimed at the Last Supper that this memorial would be carried on in a new way. Luke 22:19-20 *And he took bread, gave thanks and broke it, and gave it to them, saying, "This is my body given for you; do this in remembrance of me." In the same way, after the supper he took the cup, saying, "This cup is the new covenant in my blood, which is poured out for you."* (NIV®) Jesus identified His body and blood with the body and blood of the Passover lamb. Israel was given the Passover to remember once a year, but we have communion as a memorial which we can use to remember Jesus' sacrifice very day. In a spiritual sense, I'm eating the Lamb of God when I eat the bread of communion. I am remembering and declaring that His body was broken for **me**. His blood was shed for **my** sins. This is up close and personal, or it is only a ritual and meaningless.

God knows we need reminders. Psalm 103:14 *for he knows how we are formed, he remembers that we are dust.* (NIV®) Even as Christians, we can become so accustomed to rituals or reading or praying that they become meaningless. But God wants me to be reminded I was once on the path of destruction and that He saved me. He wants me to recall His great worth and my need for Him every day. Psalm 145:1-2 *I will exalt you, my God the King; I will praise your name for ever and ever. Every day I will praise you and extol your name for ever and ever.* (NIV®) If I were able to do as David did, praising God every day, I would be exercising my reminders. I need to take a few minutes of every day to tell God how great He is and thank Him for saving me, not only to worship Him, but also to remind myself.

There is another reason that Peter was reminding us. It is because it is the only way to ensure that Christianity lives on. Oh, yes, Jesus and the Holy Spirit would make sure it does, but they work through us to accomplish that. Even in the Old Testament, this was the way it had to be. Psalm 78:2-4 *I will open my mouth in parables, I will utter hidden things, things from of old — what we have heard and known, what our fathers have told us. We will not hide them from their children; we will tell the next generation the praiseworthy deeds of the Lord, his power, and the wonders he has done.* (NIV®) I continually need to remind myself of what God has done for me so I can tell the next generation. This is the message that Peter is echoing. It has come down from God through the ages. Remind each other how great God is. Remind each other that Jesus has died for us. Remind each other where we would be if it were not for Jesus.

Bible Myths – 2 Peter 1:16-18

For we did not follow cunningly devised fables when we made known to you the power and coming of our Lord Jesus Christ, but were eyewitnesses of His majesty. For He received from God the Father honor and glory when such a voice came to Him from the Excellent Glory: "This is My beloved Son, in whom I am well pleased." And we heard this voice which came from heaven when we were with Him on the holy mountain. (NKJV)

At one time I believed the Bible was nothing more than myths, legends, or folk tales that had been handed down from generation to generation. I took a class in college that studied folk tales. It showed how the stories developed over time. They may have started with a real incident but as they were told and retold they changed. I knew next to nothing about the Bible but believed it was no better than these folk tales.

I had heard parts of the Bible read but had never actually read it for myself. I heard about Jonah and the whale and didn't know it really is Jonah and the fish, not a whale. I heard about Jesus walking on water, His death, and resurrection. I heard about His ascension and also about His mother's ascension, which is not in the Bible. Traditions and stories have been passed down that are not in the Bible and they have changed over time. When these are mixed with the words of the Bible great confusion can result, especially if you aren't familiar with the Bible.

Peter was writing down some of his thoughts because there were already myths and stories being spread. One of these is recorded in Matthew 28:12-15 to discredit Jesus' resurrection. *When the chief priests had met with the elders and devised a plan, they gave the soldiers a large sum of money, telling them, "You are to say, 'His disciples came during the night and stole him away while we were asleep.' If this report gets to the governor, we will satisfy him and keep you out of trouble." So the soldiers took the money and did as they were instructed. And this story has been widely circulated among the Jews to this very day. (NIV®)* To a historian, it is obvious that the guards were bribed and that the governor was in on it. They were Roman guards, not the temple guards. If a Roman guard fell asleep on duty and lost his charge, he was executed. Obviously, the story that they fell asleep had to be false.

There are multiple testimonies of the Apostles and others that they saw Jesus after His death. Many witnessed His ascension into Heaven.

The myth that He wasn't resurrected is busted.

Another fable is that Jesus didn't die but fainted and was revived in the cool of the tomb and then escaped. This can be discounted by simply reading the accounts of His crucifixion. John 19:38-40 *Later, Joseph of Arimathea asked Pilate for the body of Jesus. Now Joseph was a disciple of Jesus, but secretly because he feared the Jews. With Pilate's permission, he came and took the body away. He was accompanied by Nicodemus, the man who earlier had visited Jesus at night. Nicodemus brought a mixture of myrrh and aloes, about seventy-five pounds. Taking Jesus' body, the two of them wrapped it, with the spices, in strips of linen. This was in accordance with Jewish burial customs.* (NIV®)

The first thing to note is that His body was given to these two men by Pilate. In Mark 15:43-45, we find that Joseph had to wait for Pilate to make sure Jesus was dead. The centurion who was responsible to insure Jesus' death verified it. This centurion's job was to execute people. He knew when a person was dead. We also have the testimony about His death in John 19:33-34 *But when they came to Jesus and found that he was already dead, they did not break his legs. Instead, one of the soldiers pierced Jesus' side with a spear, bringing a sudden flow of blood and water.* (NIV®) Medical facts testify that when a person dies, blood cells separate from the serum in the blood, which then will look more like water. The flow of blood and water from Jesus' side is proof He was dead.

The second thing to note is that Jesus was badly beaten. He probably had most of the skin on His back ripped off by the flogging He endured. Add to this trauma 75 pounds of spices and wrap Him up in cloth. There is no way a man could survive. Not only that, but if either of these two men would have detected any sign of breathing or heartbeat, they would have stopped. This was all observed by the women who had stayed with Him during the whole crucifixion (Luke

23:55). There was no sign of life. If He had revived in the tomb, how could He possibly unwrap Himself?

The myth that Jesus didn't really die is busted.

These myths have been busted simply by looking at a few verses in the Bible. I haven't answered the question about the reliability of the Bible but will address that next.

Biblical Accuracy – 2 Peter 1:19-21

And so we have the prophetic word made more sure, to which you do well to pay attention as to a lamp shining in a dark place, until the day dawns and the morning star arises in your hearts. But know this first of all, that no prophecy of Scripture is a matter of one's own interpretation, for no prophecy was ever made by an act of human will, but men moved by the Holy Spirit spoke from God. (NASB)

How can I determine if the Bible is reliable? Peter says in this passage that the prophecies are true. He wasn't speaking of things that are still to come in the future, but things that were predicted and had already happened. One of the biggest keys to the reliability of the Bible is the fact that prophesies were recorded and history can document they occurred as predicted. In Isaiah 42:9 God makes a clear declaration, *"See, the former things have taken place, and new things I declare; before they spring into being I announce them to you."* (NIV®) God is never afraid to make a prediction because He is all-knowing and all-powerful. He knows what will happen and He has the power to ensure that it will take place as He foretold. Isaiah 46:10 *"I make known the end from the beginning, from ancient times, what is still to come. I say: My purpose will stand, and I will do all that I please."* (NIV®)

God challenges anyone to be as accurate in their predictions as He is – 100% accurate. Isaiah 44:7 *"Who then is like me? Let him proclaim it. Let him declare and lay out before me what has happened since I established my ancient people, and what is yet to come — yes, let him foretell what will come."* (NIV®) It is easy for someone to say, "I told you so" when there is no documentation that he predicted it. However, it's another matter to write down predictions and then let everyone scrutinize the results. The Bible does just that. God has made hundreds of prophesies and many have already come true and some are for the future.

I could document many of these predictions but other authors have done much better jobs. So I will only point out one of my favorites. Daniel 9:25-*26a "Know and understand this: From the issuing of the decree to restore and rebuild Jerusalem until the Anointed One, the ruler, comes, there will be seven 'sevens,' and sixty-two 'sevens.' It will be rebuilt with streets and a trench, but in times of trouble. After the sixty-two 'sevens,' the Anointed One will be cut off and will have nothing."* (NIV®) You can do the math assuming that a "seven" is seven years and that each year uses the Jewish calendar of 360 days. The total number of "sevens" from the time that King Artaxerxes gave permission for Nehemiah to start rebuilding Jerusalem (see Nehemiah 2:4-8) until Jesus, the Anointed One, would appear is 69 or 483 Jewish years. That would be 476.3836 of our years. Artaxerxes made the proclamation in 444 B.C. So that means that in 32.3836 A.D. the Messiah (which means Anointed One) should appear and make Himself known. That just happens to be the Palm Sunday when Jesus rode into Jerusalem on a donkey.

Think about that. How could Daniel make such a precise prediction if God had not revealed it to Him? Of course, Jesus fulfilled many other prophesies made by many different people who wrote the Old Testament. I mentioned that Jesus rode on a donkey and that prophesy is found in Zechariah 9:9. Someone might argue that Jesus staged the whole thing because He knew the prophecies. However, how could he have staged the time and place of His birth? Micah 5:2 said the Messiah had to be born in Bethlehem. Since Jesus' mother was living in Nazareth when she was pregnant, it took the decree of a Roman emperor to make sure she was in Bethlehem on the right day to have Jesus born there. Augustus didn't know anything about the prophecies and certainly didn't know that Mary was pregnant and about to give birth, yet God moved him to declare a census that required Mary and Joseph to go to Bethlehem at just the right time. See Luke 2:1-7.

What about the prophecies of His death? Surely no one would want to stage His own death just to fulfill a prophecy. Psalm 22:7-8 *All who see me mock me; they hurl insults, shaking their heads: "He trusts in the Lord; let the Lord rescue him. Let him deliver him, since he delights in him."* (NIV®) This described the attitude of those who crucified Jesus. See Mark 15:31. He couldn't stage that. Psalm 22:16-18 *Dogs have surrounded me; a band of evil men has encircled me, they have pierced my hands and my feet. I can count all my bones; people stare and gloat over me. They divide my garments among them and cast lots for my clothing.* (NIV®) What is remarkable is that Jesus knew this was exactly what would be done to Him and yet He didn't attempt to stop it. He knew all the prophecies had to be fulfilled; otherwise, someone could say God was a liar when He spoke through these prophets.

When a person embraces the fact that the Bible is accurate, it doesn't take long before he finds out who Jesus is and that he needs to surrender to Him. When that happens, it is just like a lamp starting to shine in a dark place. That person is then born again and the Morning Star (Jesus) is in his heart. I know that for a fact. It happened to me.

Second Peter – Chapter Two

False Teachers – 2 Peter 2:1-3

But there were also false prophets among the people, even as there will be false teachers among you, who will secretly bring in destructive heresies, even denying the Lord who bought them, and bring on themselves swift destruction. And many will follow their destructive ways, because of whom the way of truth will be blasphemed. By covetousness they will exploit you with deceptive words; for a long time their judgment has not been idle, and their destruction does not slumber. (NKJV)

When did false teaches and prophets start leading God's people astray? They have always been with us. Their leader and instructor is Satan himself. Genesis 3:1 *Now the serpent was more crafty than any of the wild animals the Lord God had made. He said to the woman, "Did God really say, 'You must not eat from any tree in the garden'?"* (NIV®) The basis for all false teaching is that it questions the Word of God, and in doing so, questions God's character. The ultimate goal of a false teacher is to discredit God. Many are not aware of this, because they don't realize they are following Satan's lead.

An example of this is demonstrated by the wealth and prosperity teaching. The leaders proclaim that God want you to be healthy and wealthy. If you are not, then there is something wrong with your faith. However, we have Peter's clear teaching in 1 Peter 1:6-7 that tells us we will face trials in our lives to strengthen our faith. These trails are light and momentary because they only occur in this life. They are not eternal as Paul says in 2 Corinthians 4:16-18. *Therefore we do not lose heart. Though outwardly we are wasting away, yet inwardly we are being renewed day by day. For our light and momentary troubles are achieving for us an eternal glory that far outweighs them all. So we fix our eyes not on what is seen, but on what is unseen. For what is seen is temporary, but what is unseen is eternal.* (NIV®) Jesus says in Matthew 6:19-21 *"Do not lay up for yourselves treasures on earth, where moth and rust consume and where thieves break in and steal, but lay up for yourselves treasures in heaven, where neither moth nor rust consumes and where thieves do not break in and steal. For where your treasure is, there will your heart be also."* (RSV) Who is right?

Peter, Paul and Jesus, or those who say we should all be rich and prosperous? If the false teachers are right then the words of Jesus are doubtful, as well as Peter's and Paul's. We have affirmed that Scripture is from God and therefore God must be wrong if the false teachers are right. The false teachers won't say it clearly but by their teaching they are declaring God evil whenever bad things happen to people who have faith. Of course, they won't say that so instead they blame the person's faith. The faith of many people has been destroyed because they have been taught incorrectly.

What is so destructive about this or any other heresy? It does several things. For those who are Christians, it leads them down the wrong path so that their lives are consumed, not with glorifying God, but by fulfilling their own desires or their faith is destroyed as mentioned above. Satan loves this because they are so busy going the wrong direction that they don't lead others to Jesus. If their faith is destroyed then unbelievers can point to them as examples of those who now deny God. Peter says that because of them the way of truth will be blasphemed.

Just take a look at some of the stuff TV evangelists are saying and doing and you will see why non-Christians are bad-mouthing Christianity. It is evident that many are only out to make money and not tell the truth about man's sinfulness and the need for Jesus. Yes, sometimes they work that in, but many are blatantly out to make money from their "gospel." A good example is those who will send you a prayer cloth for a donation. The prayer cloth is supposed to have the same ability to heal people and answer their prayers as was found in Acts 19:11-12 *God did extraordinary miracles through Paul, so that even handkerchiefs and aprons that had touched him were taken to the sick, and their illnesses were cured and the evil spirits left them.* (NIV®) There is nothing in the Bible that says a cloth a TV preacher has touched will bring about a miracle by God in the same way.

In fact, these people should read what God's attitude is toward them. Acts 8:18-21 *When Simon saw that the Spirit was given at the laying on of the apostles' hands, he offered them money and said, "Give me also this ability so that everyone on whom I lay my hands may receive the Holy Spirit." Peter answered: "May your money perish with you, because you thought you could buy the gift of God with money! You have no part or share in this ministry, because your heart is not right before God.* (NIV®) I think it is clear that when false teachers are motivated by money, God is not pleased and they have no part in His ministry.

There is another interesting thing about false prophets. God does use them, but not in the way they think and we seldom consider this. Deuteronomy 13:1-3 *"If a prophet arises among you, or a dreamer of dreams, and gives you a sign or a wonder, and the sign or wonder which he tells you comes to pass, and if he says, 'Let us go after other gods,' which you have not known, 'and let us serve them,' you shall not listen to the words of that prophet or to that dreamer of dreams; for the Lord your God is testing you, to know whether you love the Lord your God with all your heart and with all your soul."* (RSV) I have to admit many of the false teachers on TV and other places perform miracles. The most common is that people are healed. But look carefully at these verses. God warned the Israelites that these false teachers would give signs and wonders but that their teaching was wrong. If a preacher tells us to go after other gods, wealth, power, or anything else, then we should not listen no matter how many miracles they do. God is testing us with these false teacher to see if we will read His Word and find out from Him what He wants us to do and how to act. When we listen to those false teachers and put things other than God first, we will reap the consequences of our actions – ruined lives and loss of rewards in heaven. See 1 Corinthians 3 :10-15.

If we follow false teachers and lose our rewards, what will happen to the false teachers? I guess it depends on whether or not they really know Jesus or not. If they do, then they too will lose their rewards. If we are His children then this verse may apply to those who lead us astray. Matthew 18:6 *But if anyone causes one of these little ones who believe in me to sin, it would be better for him to have a large millstone hung around his neck and to be drowned in the depths of the sea.* (NIV®) That sounds quite severe to me. Peter also confirms that they will not go without punishment. As a teacher, I don't ever want to lead anyone astray.

Condemnation or Rescue – 2 Peter 2:4-10a

For if God did not spare angels when they sinned, but sent them to hell, putting them into gloomy dungeons to be held for judgment; if he did not spare the ancient world when he brought the flood on its ungodly people, but protected Noah, a preacher of righteousness, and seven others; if he condemned the cities of Sodom and Gomorrah by burning them to ashes, and made them an example of what is going to happen to the ungodly; and if he rescued Lot, a righteous man, who was distressed by the filthy lives of lawless men (for that righteous man, living among them day after day, was tormented in his righteous soul by the lawless deeds he saw and heard)— if this is so, then the Lord knows how to rescue godly men from trials and to hold the unrighteous for the day of judgment, while continuing their punishment. This is especially true of those who follow the corrupt desire of the sinful nature and despise authority. (NIV®)

It's pretty hard to escape the primary message of these seven verses. It's also very easy to focus on the judgment and punishment of sinners and miss the message of rescue for the righteous person. It is a message of contrasts. If you take away the condemnation of the wicked, then the impact of rescue is significantly diminished.

One of the big problems with the way we communicate the message of salvation today is that we are afraid to tell people hell is a real place and that people who are not righteous will go there when they die. It isn't popular and one reason is that it is politically incorrect to let people know that certain behavior is sin. Most people will agree that the big one is sin. That would be murder. However it is increasingly difficult to convince anyone that the little ones are sin. Adultery used to be a big one, but even now it is accepted as long as those involved have found their "soul mates." Go through the Ten Commandments and murder is just about the only one that most people universally agree is wrong. However, there are some religions and cultures where murder is ok as long as it isn't against members of their own tribe or religious belief.

The truth is, from God's viewpoint, sin is sin. While one sin may be more heinous than another, it only takes one, small or large, to cause a person to be judged in violation of His laws. James 2:10-11 *For whoever keeps the whole law but fails in one point has become guilty of all of it. For he who said, "Do not commit adultery," said also, "Do not kill." If you do not commit adultery but do kill, you have become a transgressor of the law.* (RSV) The point is that any transgression against God will condemn a person as unrighteous, and as Peter so clearly pointed out, God knows how to make sure they are punished.

If it were not for the clear punishment for sin, some people would never repent and look for the rescue. This brings up another reason why preaching hell, fire, and brimstone is not popular. Somehow, modern Christians have gotten the idea that fear of punishment isn't a valid reason for salvation. They think that a person should turn to Jesus because of His great love and mercy for us. Therefore, they don't tell others about His punishment for sin; otherwise, they might only come to Christ for "fire insurance" and not out of a desire to obey and love God. They are afraid that coming only to escape punishment will result in worldly Christians who continue in their sin, believing that they are covered and won't be punished.

We should not eliminate preaching hell, fire, and brimstone based on this misguided concept. Each person who comes to Christ is a spiritual baby and must learn and grow. The one who comes out of fear of punishment must grow in his love of God. The one who comes because of God's love must grow in his obedience and fear of God; otherwise, he might assume that out of God's love, every sin will be excused. Generally, neither of these categories of people languishes in sin but grow and become more Christ-like.

What about this rescue Peter mentions? He repeats that God rescues the righteous. What about Lot? Read the account of how the two angels had to drag him out of the city. Genesis 19:16 *But he hesitated. So the men seized his hand and the hand of his wife and the hands of his two daughters, for the compassion of the Lord was upon him; and they brought him out, and put him outside the city.* (NASB) Lot was captivated by his life in the wicked city. He hesitated leaving, but God had compassion on him. How different am I from Lot or those who were destroyed in Sodom and Gomorra? Is it possible that every single person in those cities were engaged in the sinful behavior that was described? Probably not, but they were still sinners. God had earlier said that He would spare the cities if only ten righteous people were found (Genesis 18:32) and obviously He didn't find ten.

God rescued Lot in spite of his attachment to the sinful cities. He declared Lot a righteous person. This should stop and make me think about how righteous I am. Isaiah 64:6 *All of us have become like one who is unclean, and all our righteous acts are like filthy rags; we all*

shrivel up like a leaf, and like the wind our sins sweep us away.
(NIV®) I can't claim any righteousness on my own. There is only one
way I can be classified as righteous and that is when God says I am. I
deserve the same punishment as the people in Sodom and Gomorrah.
However, God has chosen me and declared me righteous. Why would
He do that?

Romans 3:21-26 *But now a righteousness from God, apart from
law, has been made known, to which the Law and the Prophets testify.
This righteousness from God comes through faith in Jesus Christ to
all who believe. There is no difference, for all have sinned and fall
short of the glory of God, and are justified freely by his grace through
the redemption that came by Christ Jesus. God presented him as a
sacrifice of atonement, through faith in his blood. He did this to
demonstrate his justice, because in his forbearance he had left the
sins committed beforehand unpunished—he did it to demonstrate his
justice at the present time, so as to be just and the one who justifies
those who have faith in Jesus.* (NIV®)

God declares me righteous not because of anything I've done. He
does it to demonstrate His justice and His mercy. Anytime I start to
think that I deserved rescue I need to remember that without God
giving me faith to believe, I never would (Ephesians 2:8-9). I can't
boast before God in any way, shape, or form. I can only be thankful
for His rescue and be obedient to Him since I owe Him my life.

Be Careful Who You Slander – 2 Peter 2:10-12

*This is especially true of those who follow the corrupt desire of
the sinful nature and despise authority. Bold and arrogant, these men
are not afraid to slander celestial beings; yet even angels, although
they are stronger and more powerful, do not bring slanderous
accusations against such beings in the presence of the Lord. But these
men blaspheme in matters they do not understand. They are like brute
beasts, creatures of instinct, born only to be caught and destroyed,
and like beasts they too will perish.* (NIV®)

I'll have to backtrack just a little because Peter jumps from
making sure we know that there will be a judgment for unrighteous
people to some specifics about their behavior. He lists two general
categories, those following the corrupt desire of the sinful nature and

those who despise authority. He first expands on the second, despising authority.

These are false teachers who think they have it all figured out but really don't understand spiritual things. If they did, they wouldn't be so bold or arrogant. They have their own understanding of the structure of spiritual authority. According to the Holy Spirit, who is speaking the word of God through Peter, they are way off-base.

The celestial beings these men slander are not the angels or God Himself. Peter makes that clear. That leaves only the forces of evil that they slander. Paul gives us a hint of their authority structure. Ephesians 6:12 *For we are not contending against flesh and blood, but against the principalities, against the powers, against the world rulers of this present darkness, against the spiritual hosts of wickedness in the heavenly places.* (RSV) They have principalities. The Encarta Dictionary[8] is quite helpful. It says, "The position or jurisdiction of a prince." So the forces of evil are structured with rulers, implying there are a bunch of dukes and lower officials followed up by the peons who do all the dirty work. The Encarta Dictionary also defines principality as, "an angel of the third of the nine orders of angels in the traditional Christian hierarchy." Don't ask me where they came up with this tradition but it fits with the concept.

Another thing to remember is that these beings have access to God. Revelation 12:9-10 says that Satan finally gets tossed out of heaven but it also says that he accuses the saints before God day and night. The book of Job confirms Satan not only has access to God but that he is free to visit earth. Job 1:7 *The Lord said to Satan, "Where have you come from?" Satan answered the Lord, "From roaming through the earth and going back and forth in it."* (NIV®) The book of Job verifies that Satan has no power except that which God allows.

This is also demonstrated in 1 Kings 22:19-24. The prophet Micaiah relates his vision in which God is seated before the heavenly hosts. Some are on the left and others on the right. God asks for someone to entice Ahab. One spirit comes and says he will be a lying spirit in the mouth of the false prophets. God sends him to do it. The

---

[8] Encarta® World English Dictionary [North American Edition] © & (P)2009 Microsoft Corporation. All rights reserved. Developed for Microsoft by Bloomsbury Publishing Plc.

false prophet, Zedekiah, has no clue that his prophecies are from an evil being.

This glimpse into the heavenly realms is a key to what Peter is talking about. Examine 1 Kings 22:22. *And the Lord said to him, 'By what means?' And he said, 'I will go forth, and will be a lying spirit in the mouth of all his prophets.' And he said, 'You are to entice him, and you shall succeed; go forth and do so.'* (RSV) God's sovereignty is evident in His command to the evil spirit. If a person starts ranting and raving against spiritual beings, telling them what to do and where to go and calling them names (you can see some of this on TV), then there is a risk he is actually countermanding the will of God.

Take David's example when he was fleeing from Jerusalem. Shimei cursed David and threw rocks and dirt at him. When David's bodyguard wanted to kill Shimei, David didn't let him. 2 Samuel 16:10 *But the king said, "What do you and I have in common, you sons of Zeruiah? If he is cursing because the Lord said to him, 'Curse David,' who can ask, 'Why do you do this?'"* (NIV®) Now Shimei was not a celestial being but David recognized this could have been from the Lord. Am I so confident I know the mind of the Lord that I can go around commanding each and every spirit what to do?

There are several examples in the Bible which allow us to take command over evil spirits. I won't talk about Jesus because He knew the perfect will of the Father. However, He did say those who believe would drive out demons (Mark 16:17). He also said in the following verse that we would pick up snakes, drink deadly poison without harm, and place our hands on the sick and heal them. Certainly the book of Acts records many demons being cast out. Does this mean that every person will do these things? I don't think so and I'm not going to tempt God by drinking poison to prove I believe, and I'm also going to be careful about what I say to spirits.

If I see a person whom I suspect is demon possessed, will I attempt to cast out the demon? I guess that depends on how the Holy Spirit moves me at the time. What if that demon has been allowed to bring that person to repentance (1 Corinthians 5:1-5) and I cast it out before it has been allowed to do its work? Am I not thwarting the hand of God? If I do decide to do something, then I need to take these passages to heart and do it with respect to authority and not slander the demon.

Jude tells exactly how to do it as he uses some of the same words as Peter. Jude 8-9 *In the very same way, these dreamers pollute their own bodies, reject authority and slander celestial beings. But even the archangel Michael, when he was disputing with the devil about the body of Moses, did not dare to bring a slanderous accusation against him, but said, "The Lord rebuke you!"* (NIV®)

What did I learn from all of this?

There are spiritual battles and forces in the heavenly realms which are far beyond my understanding.

People who venture into them with the wrong attitude are going to end up getting burned.

God is sovereign, even over these forces.

If I should not slander these beings, then how much more should I be careful talking about the ones they control – like leaders of nations.

Don't Become Part of the Accursed Brood – 2 Peter 2:13-16

They will be paid back with harm for the harm they have done. Their idea of pleasure is to carouse in broad daylight. They are blots and blemishes, reveling in their pleasures while they feast with you. With eyes full of adultery, they never stop sinning; they seduce the unstable; they are experts in greed — an accursed brood! They have left the straight way and wandered off to follow the way of Balaam son of Beor, who loved the wages of wickedness. But he was rebuked for his wrongdoing by a donkey — a beast without speech — who spoke with a man's voice and restrained the prophet's madness. (NIV®)

Peter continues to warn us about false prophets and teachers who would lead us astray if they could. We need to be alert by observing their actions in public and elsewhere. Peter warns that they carouse in broad daylight. This simply means that they don't try to hide their immoral behavior. It could be drinking, partying, or sexual immorality. They really don't care what others think of their behavior. People who call themselves Christians and worse, Christian leaders, who do this give Christianity a bad name. Jesus said in Matthew 7:20 *"Thus you will know them by their fruits."* (RSV) Peter does a good job describing their fruit. They seem to fall into two areas, sexual sin and greed.

It isn't just false prophets that fall into these sins. You can probably list several prominent Christian leaders who have had the same problem. The only difference between them and the false prophets is that they did it in secret, but it was exposed and then they fell from their position. So without dwelling on either the false teachers or the fallen Christian leaders, perhaps I should look inside and see if I am susceptible to the same sins, whether they are committed in secret or in public.

What about these eyes that are full of adultery? How do I stack up in this area? Job 31:1 *I made a covenant with mine eyes; why then should I think upon a maid?* (KJV) After looking at different versions and the original Hebrew, I think that the KJV did the best job translating this verse. Job wasn't talking about just seeing someone or glancing, but looking, then thinking and letting his mind engage in knowing all about this maid. The warning in James 1:14 comes to mind, *but each one is tempted when, by his own evil desire, he is dragged away and enticed.* (NIV®)

Our society is in almost total acceptance that either sex can look all they want as long as they don't touch. That is filthy hogwash! Peter says the next step is to seduce the unstable. James says that it gives birth to sin. Jesus also commented on it. Matthew 6:22-23 *"The eye is the lamp of the body. If your eyes are good, your whole body will be full of light. But if your eyes are bad, your whole body will be full of darkness. If then the light within you is darkness, how great is that darkness!"* (NIV®) What I allow myself to see and dwell upon can lead to light or darkness. If I let my eyes constantly view sexually explicit images, I will have a lustful heart leading to lustful practices. If I watch violence and play games of violence, then my heart will become accustomed to it and want more. This can easily turn into violent behavior; road rage, for example. If I read good books and watch uplifting movies, then I will have light in my heart leading to a life more pleasing to the Lord.

In Numbers 22, God gave us Balaam as an unusual example. He is a confusing figure because he actually talks with God, as did many of the O.T. prophets. He obeys God, at first. Yet when the emissaries from Balak return, he doesn't tell them he can't go with them but asks them to stay the night so he can see what God will say. He doesn't take God at His word but wants to double check to see if there is a way he might get some money from these Moabites. Strangely

129

enough, God lets him go with Balak's people in order to curse Israel.
But God also tries to kill him on the way. Obviously, God could have
killed him, but it served as a warning that Balaam must speak only
what God wants. And Balaam does speak what God wanted. He
blesses Israel four times over and finally ends up cursing Israel's
enemies.

You would think Balaam would be listed as an example to follow,
but that isn't so. Later references to Balaam in the Bible are bad. Here
was a guy who was in communion with God but let his greed get the
best of him. It isn't explained when he did it, but Balaam counseled
Moab how to infiltrate Israel and draw them away from God. Greed
can do that to any of us. It may not be greed for money, but for power,
my own time, or my own space. I think – just a little more time at
work and then I'll read the Bible or pray. A little more TV and then
I'll pray. I can even pursue good things like exercise or community
service and neglect time with the Lord. The pull of the world is so
strong that I must constantly be alert to the things that would draw me
away from God. I don't think Balaam set out to be classified with an
accursed brood but that's where he ended up.

When God speaks clearly and I know what He has said, I need not
look for any way out. In 1 Kings 13 there is an interesting story of a
prophet from Judah who was plainly told by God to go to Israel, make
a prophesy over the alter that King Jeroboam had built, then go home
without eating or drinking in Israel. A second, older prophet in Israel
lies to the first and tells him that God said to eat and drink with him,
so the first does, but it cost him his life.

Balaam lost his life because of his attempt to get around the clear
blessings God had given Israel through him. The prophet from Judah
died because he listened to someone who countermanded God's clear
instruction. I need to make sure I'm listening to God and can
recognize His voice (know the Bible) vs. the voice of false teachers. If
I don't, the consequences could be deadly.

Unstable Leaders – 2 Peter 2:17-19

*These are springs without water, and mists driven by a storm, for
whom the black darkness has been reserved. For speaking out
arrogant words of vanity they entice by fleshly desires, by sensuality,*

those who barely escape from the ones who live in error, promising them freedom while they themselves are slaves of corruption; for by what a man is overcome, by this he is enslaved. (NASB)

We are continuing to discus people who follow corrupt desires, slander celestial beings, carouse, are adulterous, seduce the unstable, and a bunch of other things. These are people who call themselves Christians and some even become leaders in their church.

Make no mistake, they are not Christians and never have been. The opening of verse 17 verifies this. They are springs without water. Jesus made it clear that Christians are springs of living water. John 7:37-39 *On the last and greatest day of the Feast, Jesus stood and said in a loud voice, "If anyone is thirsty, let him come to me and drink. Whoever believes in me, as the Scripture has said, streams of living water will flow from within him." By this he meant the Spirit, whom those who believed in him were later to receive. Up to that time the Spirit had not been given, since Jesus had not yet been glorified.* (NIV®)

Ezekiel describes a vision of the temple during the millennium reign of Christ. In chapter 47, he describes the water that flows from the temple. Zechariah 14:8 says it will be a river of living water. Ezekiel says the living water gets deeper and deeper as it flows from the temple. This is the way it is with God's Spirit living in us. It continues to flow to others and as it does, it multiplies and becomes deeper. This does not occur with the unstable because not only do they not have living water, they have no water at all.

Ezekiel says there are trees beside the river. Revelation 22:1-3 says that these trees beside the river of life will bring healing to the nations. The Holy Spirit living in me should not bring contention but healing. Unstable people who Peter describes bring strife and anger. They stir up emotions by proclaiming everyone should have certain rights and should protect those rights. They ignore Scripture such as this: Philippians 2:3-5 *Do nothing out of selfish ambition or vain conceit, but in humility consider others better than yourselves. Each of you should look not only to your own interests, but also to the interests of others. Your attitude should be the same as that of Christ Jesus:* (NIV®)

What is Jesus' attitude? How should I protect my rights and my freedoms? Should I follow the advice of talk show host or that of Jesus? Consider the fruitful lives of these unstable people, some of whom have been married multiple times. Consider what Jesus said. Matthew 5:38-42 *"You have heard that it was said, 'Eye for eye, and tooth for tooth.' But I tell you, do not resist an evil person. If someone strikes you on the right cheek, turn to him the other also. And if someone wants to sue you and take your tunic, let him have your cloak as well. If someone forces you to go one mile, go with him two miles. Give to the one who asks you, and do not turn away from the one who wants to borrow from you."* (NIV®) Do unstable people proclaim help for the downtrodden or a me-first attitude? They appeal to the vanity of their followers.

The living water flows from the temple and into the Dead Sea. Ezekiel 47:9 *Swarms of living creatures will live wherever the river flows. There will be large numbers of fish, because this water flows there and makes the salt water fresh; so where the river flows everything will live.* (NIV®) Remember that Jesus said we would be fishers of men. Do I bring life to people or death? Does my attitude turn people off or let them see the love of Jesus? Unstable counselors only breed unstable followers, people who become anxious about the future instead of embracing the opportunities to share the Gospel. They become anxious about the economy instead of trusting God in all circumstances. The unstable leaders prosper at the expense of their disciples.

They are enslaved by their own passions and seek to enslave others as well. Of course, they claim it is for the best for the nation. They claim it is patriotic. However, they are enslaved to their ideals. Their ideals prevent them from living a life free in Christ. Romans 6:22 *But now that you have been set free from sin and have become slaves of God, the return you get is sanctification and its end, eternal life.* (RSV) What do you want to do? Do you want to be a slave to the anxiety the world is pumping out or do you want to be free to do what God wants?

Once Saved always Saved? – 2 Peter 2:20-22

For if after they have escaped the defilements of the world by the knowledge of the Lord and Savior Jesus Christ, they are again entangled in them and are overcome, the last state has become worse for them than the first. For it would be better for them not to have known the way of righteousness, than having known it, to turn away from the holy commandment delivered to them. It has happened to them according to the true proverb, "A dog returns to its own vomit," and, "A sow, after washing, returns to wallowing in the mire." (NASB)

As someone who believes that once a person has been saved they can't lose their salvation, this verse stops to make me think. There are several verses in the Bible that say almost the same thing. However, I do believe that God doesn't contradict Himself, especially in matters as important as this. I'll list a couple of passages that appear to support the position that Christians can lose their salvation.

Hebrews 6:4-6 *It is impossible for those who have once been enlightened, who have tasted the heavenly gift, who have shared in the Holy Spirit, who have tasted the goodness of the word of God and the powers of the coming age, if they fall away, to be brought back to repentance, because to their loss they are crucifying the Son of God all over again and subjecting him to public disgrace.* (NIV®)

Hebrews 10:26-27 *If we deliberately keep on sinning after we have received the knowledge of the truth, no sacrifice for sins is left, but only a fearful expectation of judgment and of raging fire that will consume the enemies of God.* (NIV®)

These verses all have at their heart a condition – the word if – and some requirements. There are two requirements; falling away in some manner and what appears to be a description of initial salvation. In Peter, initial salvation is the description of a person having the knowledge of the Lord and Savior Jesus. In Hebrews, it is being enlightened and tasting the heavenly gift and receiving the knowledge of the truth.

The verses in Hebrews 10 are followed by verses 32-39, which remind the believers what they have already gone through. This is fruit inspection. There is no indication that these people have fallen away. It ends with Hebrews 10:39 *But we are not of those who shrink back and are destroyed, but of those who believe and are saved.* (NIV®) Salvation is clearly linked to believing and good works are the proof of salvation. This passage is then reminding us that a person who is truly saved is not going to continue sinning and therefore will not be condemned. This passage is all about what a person does with the knowledge of the truth. If it goes into the heart and finds good soil, it produces good fruit. In other words, just knowing the truth doesn't mean one follows or even believes it. Romans 10:9 shows that belief is required to be saved. *That if you confess with your mouth, "Jesus is Lord," and believe in your heart that God raised him from the dead, you will be saved.* (NIV®) When put in context, Hebrews 10:26-27 doesn't support a Christian losing salvation.

Hebrews 6:4-6 is a bit tougher to handle because of the many references to what appears as salvation. What does enlightened, tasting the heavenly gift, sharing in the Holy Spirit, tasting the goodness of the Word of God and powers of the coming age all mean? Well, it fits the same pattern as Hebrews 10:26-39. Reading beyond, you can see the writer referring to land that soaks up God's blessings but yields bad fruit. All these blessings mentioned in verse Hebrews 6:4-5 are like the rain God sends on the good and bad land. All these are things are available to people whether or not they are Christians. I am saying that non-Christians can be enlightened. They know the truth but don't believe. They taste the heavenly gift because they are strictly following legalistic righteousness which helps them live healthy, well-balanced lives. But they don't believe in Jesus. When the Holy Spirit convicts them of sinful behavior, they straighten up but still don't believe. They can even quote Scripture and know what happens when Jesus comes back, but deep down in their hearts they don't believe. They are Pharisees. These verses don't support a Christian losing salvation but simply points out that people can be outwardly righteous but not saved. Talk to anyone in a cult, especially the ones who are outwardly squeaky clean. You would think they are saved.

Jesus put it this way: Matthew 12:43-45 *"When an evil spirit comes out of a man, it goes through arid places seeking rest and does not find it. Then it says, 'I will return to the house I left.' When it arrives, it finds the house unoccupied, swept clean and put in order. Then it goes and takes with it seven other spirits more wicked than itself, and they go in and live there. And the final condition of that man is worse than the first. That is how it will be with this wicked generation."* (NIV®) When a person is self righteous but not saved, he is like this man, clean but empty. If he were saved, he would have the Holy Spirit inside and would be protected (Ephesians 1:13).

Jesus also said: John 5:24 *"I tell you the truth, whoever hears my word and believes him who sent me has eternal life and will not be*

condemned; he has crossed over from death to life." John 10:27-30
"My sheep listen to my voice; I know them, and they follow me. I give them eternal life, and they shall never perish; no one can snatch them out of my hand. My Father, who has given them to me, is greater than all; no one can snatch them out of my Father's hand. I and the Father are one." (NIV®) If a person has truly believed, then he has received eternal life. If a person could believe and then lose salvation, Jesus would have had to say that they have life for a while or life as long as they don't screw up. If a person could lose his salvation, then Jesus would have had to say no one except that person could snatch them out of His hand. If a person could do something to lose salvation, then that would make the person greater than God the Father and Jesus.

You may ask about all those verses that talk about persevering to the end. There are many. I think all of these can be seen as a warning to those who want to judge others in regard to their Christian faith. We can't ever know if a person is saved or not. We can look at their lives and guess. When they reach the end and remain faithful, we can assume they are safely in heaven. They also serve to remind us to examine ourselves and not give up.

It is personal application time, time to examine ourselves and see if we really believe or not. If I do believe, is what I do consistent with what I believe, or am I only like land that has received rain from above but I've never surrendered completely to Jesus? (Surrender is unconditional. If it is conditional then it isn't surrender.) I'm sure there are many who enjoy the benefits of good clean living but don't know Jesus personally. They know all about Jesus, His death for our sins, His resurrection, and even His coming again. But somewhere that head knowledge has not been translated to heart knowledge or belief that saves.

Second Peter – Chapter Three

Wholesome Thinking – 2 Peter 3:1-2

Dear friends, this is now my second letter to you. I have written both of them as reminders to stimulate you to wholesome thinking. I want you to recall the words spoken in the past by the holy prophets and the command given by our Lord and Savior through your apostles. (NIV®)

What kind of thinking is wholesome? Obviously, Peter believed that God's Word as it has been given to us in the Bible can stimulate wholesome thinking. He included the Old and New Testaments by mentioning both the prophets and the apostles. In verses 15 and 16, he also includes Paul as he calls Paul's writings Scripture.

Wholesome thinking is not easy. Philippians 4:8 *Finally, brethren, whatever is true, whatever is honorable, whatever is just, whatever is pure, whatever is lovely, whatever is gracious, if there is any excellence, if there is anything worthy of praise, think about these things.* (RSV) I firmly believe that this verse is a key to transforming our minds from impurity, hate, unforgiveness, and many other things that bog us down with unwholesome thinking. Unwholesome thinking bogs us down and prevents us from having peace. When we replace these evil thoughts with the ones Paul lists, we are able to transform our minds.

However, Peter had more in mind than just thinking good thoughts since he continued on to talk about end times and how we should live in light of what God has revealed. Wholesome thinking in this case is developing a worldview that looks at all the circumstances surrounding us and then deciding on a Christian response. So we need to take the things from Philippians 4:8 and apply them. For instance, Paul says, "Whatever is just and gracious." How do we mix justice and grace together? Jesus did it by dying for our sins so we wouldn't have to. Are we willing to sacrifice ourselves not only to see justice done but also to extend grace? For example, how do we in the U.S. maintain justice with illegal immigrants and also offer grace? All I hear from the conservative right is a cry for justice which equates to carrying out the letter of the law (deportation, imprisonment, denying medical treatment) without any consideration for the fact that human beings are suffering or in need. Doesn't wholesome thinking include Jesus' words? Matthew 25:40 *"The King will reply, 'I tell you the truth, whatever you did for one of the least of these brothers of mine, you did for me.'"* (NIV®)

Take taxation as another circumstance that we all face. How does wholesome thinking apply to the way our government taxes us and provides services with those taxes? Should our response be to constantly vote against taxes? Should we criticize our politicians because they have voted for taxes? Perhaps we should consider that schools, highways, police forces, fire protection and many more blessings are provided by taxation before we demand that taxes be lowered. If we pushed tax reductions to the limits, who would provide for these services? What happened to Romans 13:6-7? *This is also why you pay taxes, for the authorities are God's servants, who give their full time to governing. Give everyone what you owe him: If you owe taxes, pay taxes; if revenue, then revenue; if respect, then respect; if honor, then honor.* (NIV®)

We have become a society that demands our rights. Our thinking has been so saturated with this concept that we believe anything and everything is a right. Is this wholesome thinking? Is demanding our rights looking at the world with a Christian attitude? Where would we be if Jesus decided His rights were more important than saving us? Matthew 5:40-41 *And if someone wants to sue you and take your tunic, let him have your cloak as well. If someone forces you to go one mile, go with him two miles.* (NIV®) That is radical thinking. It is thinking that puts the rights of other above our own rights. Dare I say it is wholesome thinking?

Personally, I have a hard time getting my mind around it all. When I read the Sermon on the Mount in Matthew 5, there is so much there that just doesn't make human sense. And that is just the point. It isn't human sense; it is divine sense. If I want to be more like Jesus, then I have to be less like the world. I must have an eternal perspective while my feet are stuck in the mud of this world. I'm nowhere near where I should be, but I hope to get further. Philippians 3:13-14 *Brothers, I do not consider myself yet to have taken hold of it. But one thing I do: Forgetting what is behind and straining toward what is ahead, I press on toward the goal to win the prize for which God has called me heavenward in Christ Jesus.* (NIV®) I want to be like Paul, but I can't even say I'm straining toward the goal and pressing on. I'm plodding along. I would like to say I have more answers but instead, I have more questions.

How about you? Are you straining toward the goal? Are you thinking wholesomely or worldly? Are you letting the Word of God transform your thinking and following it up with action in accordance with His Word or are you letting the radical right, liberal left, or mundane middle formulate your thinking and actions? I certainly hope and pray that we all can respond the way Jesus wants.

Will Jesus Return? – 2 Peter 3:3-7

Know this first of all, that in the last days mockers will come with their mocking, following after their own lusts, and saying, "Where is the promise of His coming? For ever since the fathers fell asleep, all continues just as it was from the beginning of creation." For when they maintain this, it escapes their notice that by the word of God the heavens existed long ago and the earth was formed out of water and by water, through which the world at that time was destroyed, being flooded with water. But the present heavens and earth by His word are being reserved for fire, kept for the day of judgment and destruction of ungodly men. (NASB)

Peter believed it is very important for us to remember that people will always mock Christianity. One of the seemingly easy points to mock is the promise of Jesus' return. As each year passes, it outwardly seems that they are right. How many generations have passed on since Jesus was taken up into heaven? I've even heard Christians who are very devout doubt His return could be very soon. Some even think that only spiritually immature Christians look for His return each day. Human logic tells us that if He has waited this long, then His return is not likely to be today. Is this not mocking His promise? Spiritual logic tells us to look at all the promises and keep watching; it could be today.

Perhaps one of the reason we doubt Jesus' return could be eminent is that He made it clear we can't predict when He will return. Acts 1:7 *He said to them: "It is not for you to know the times or dates the Father has set by his own authority."* (NIV®) I think He has kept us from knowing when He will return for a very good reason. We would all become lazy and irresponsible if we knew the exact date. If it were two months and three days from now, how many of us would continue our work, get our paychecks, and calculate when we could quit work but still provide for the last few days? Some might even take on debt knowing they wouldn't have to repay it. Jesus addressed this attitude in a parable. Matthew 24:45-46 *"Who then is the faithful and wise servant, whom the master has put in charge of the servants in his household to give them their food at the proper time? It will be good for that servant whose master finds him doing so when he returns."* (NIV®) He put it in a positive light – it will be good for us to continue to be good witnesses and do what He expects right up to the moment He returns.

On the other hand, the philosophy that He will not return right away produces another kind of abuse which is more in line with the mocker's attitude. Matthew 24:48-50 *"But suppose that servant is wicked and says to himself, 'My master is staying away a long time,' and he then begins to beat his fellow servants and to eat and drink with drunkards. The master of that servant will come on a day when he does not expect him and at an hour he is not aware of."* (NIV®) While this servant obviously was doing evil things, am I any different when I become negligent in my Christian duties because I don't think He is coming back immediately? Do I lose the desire to witness to others because I think I may have plenty of time? Do I not share my wealth generously to help the poor and spread the Gospel because I'm concerned that He won't come back soon and I need to save it all for my retirement?

When people say that Jesus' return isn't going to happen or even that it couldn't happen today, they are calling God a liar. Peter addresses the basis of this lie in the denial of creation. Sure, everyone believes that something happened to cause everything to come together in what we call the universe. However, they deny that it was God. The NASB says it escapes their notice. The NIV® says they deliberately forget. The Greek says they were willingly ignorant. What this means is that they choose to ignore what is before them. Romans 1:20 *For since the creation of the world God's invisible qualities — his eternal power and divine nature — have been clearly seen, being understood from what has been made, so that men are without excuse.* (NIV®) Creation points people to God and He is evident in creation unless someone doesn't want to be accountable to God.

In Genesis 1:3-31 a phrase is repeated six times. He says there was an evening and a morning, a day (first, second and so on). The word for day can be translated as a literal day or figuratively as any space of time. However, when used figuratively, there is a different form of the word or adverb to clarify the length of time. This is not the case in Genesis 1:3-31. The word has no modifiers and we see the phrase "evening and morning." There can be only one interpretation for this. Each day of creation was one day or 24 hours. Genesis has long been the focal point of scoffers when they try to disprove the Bible. They know that if they can get you to doubt the very beginning of what God has said, then you will also question other parts. The result is a faith that picks and chooses what it wants to believe. This kind of faith allows many people to call themselves Christians without surrendering themselves to Jesus. (Not really saved.) It also produces weak Christians who can rationalize sinful behavior.

Sinful behavior is also what causes us to ignore the fact that the earth was once destroyed by water. Even though the physics of erosion point to a massive flood and release of those waters, people still believe that the earth is very old and the mountains and valleys were created by eons of erosion. They don't want to accept that God caused the destruction of the earth because of man's sinfulness. If they did admit it, then they would have to admit they, too, are sinners and justifiably condemned without Jesus.

Finally we need to understand that this earth isn't all there is. It is temporary and not where we should focus our lives. Yes, we need to live here but if our ultimate goals are here, then we will be sorely disappointed. We were made for eternity, a new heaven, and a new earth. Peter reminds us that ultimately the earth will be destroyed in fire. The only thing keeping it together is God's word. We need to store up our best treasures for the real future, not the one that will be destroyed.

Bubble Theology – 2 Peter 3:8-9

But do not let this one fact escape your notice, beloved, that with the Lord one day is as a thousand years, and a thousand years as one day. The Lord is not slow about His promise, as some count slowness, but is patient toward you, not wishing for any to perish but for all to come to repentance. (NASB)

Previously in Scripture, God's eternal nature has been expressed in a forward direction. Psalm 90:4 *For a thousand years in your sight are like a day that has just gone by, or like a watch in the night.* (NIV®) This is expressed in human terms to emphasize that time passes quickly for God. However, as Peter expressed it, time can also pass slowly for Him. Again, this is put in human terms. If we examine this closely, we will understand that God is really outside of time. Time does not pass for Him. The beginning of creation is just as current to Him as the end. Every part of history and every part of the future is "now" to Him.

We can't understand the concept of existence without time. When we speak of eternity, our minds think about living forever. We still think in terms of time. God says that we can't really understand it. Ecclesiastes 3:11b *He has also set eternity in the hearts of men; yet they cannot fathom what God has done from beginning to end.* (NIV®) We think of time, life, existence as a string. It has a starting point and an ending point. I imagine that eternity is more like a soap bubble floating in the air. Always changing but no beginning or ending point. Perhaps God has stretched a string on the bubble which He calls time. As the bubble swirls and changes the string will disappear and no longer exist. In the meantime, we live our lives as if the string were the only thing that exists. We cannot fathom the rest of the bubble – eternity where God lives.

God's eternality can't be separated from His sovereignty, His omniscience, or His omnipotence. Isaiah 46:10-*11 I make known the end from the beginning, from ancient times, what is still to come. I say: My purpose will stand, and I will do all that I please. From the east I summon a bird of prey; from a far-off land, a man to fulfill my purpose. What I have said, that will I bring about; what I have planned, that will I do.* (NIV®) He puts everything in terms we can understand by speaking of beginnings and endings. Not only does God know what will happen in the future, but He is also the one who makes sure it will happen since that is His plan.

We are usually comfortable thinking God can cause animals to do what He wants, as with the bird of prey in the verse above. However, we often object to the thought that He gets people to do what He wants unless they know Him. There are many examples in the Bible where people accomplished His will without knowing it. Joseph's brothers sold him into slavery in Egypt in their desire to get rid of him. They were carrying out their own wicked schemes, but what did Joseph say about it? Genesis 50:20 *You intended to harm me, but God intended it for good to accomplish what is now being done, the saving of many lives.* (NIV®) Joseph's brothers didn't have any idea that they were actually doing what God wanted.

God hardened Pharaoh's heart so the exodus from Egypt would occur as He promised. The people in Canaan fought against Joshua because it was God's will. Joshua 11:20 *For it was the Lord himself who hardened their hearts to wage war against Israel, so that he might destroy them totally, exterminating them without mercy, as the Lord had commanded Moses.* (NIV®)

This brings me to the point of considering God's patience. When I don't understand His ways, it is easy to say that He isn't keeping His promises. When Jesus doesn't come back when I expect, I have to remember that He has a very specific reason. He knows exactly who is going to be saved from the beginning to the end. Ephesians 1:4-5 *For he chose us in him before the creation of the world to be holy and blameless in his sight. In love he predestined us to be adopted as his sons through Jesus Christ ...* (NIV®) If God is delaying the time of Jesus' return, it is only because there are still people who need to be saved.

They may not even be born yet, but He knows them as if they were alive today. Jeremiah 1:5 *"Before I formed you in the womb I knew you, before you were born I set you apart; I appointed you as a prophet to the nations."* (NIV®) Jeremiah had a specific job to do as a prophet of God. If God knew him before he was born, doesn't it make sense that He knows each of us? If He had a plan for Jeremiah, doesn't it also make sense He has a plan for us?

There is also a paradox in Peter's statement. Peter says that God wants everyone to come to repentance and be saved. Yet it is clear that many people reject God and are not saved. This is a mystery that has no answer on our little string. If I could see the bubble, and someday I will, I would be able to understand. For now I know this. He saved me and it isn't because of anything I did. I don't deserve it. Because of this, I worship and adore Him.

Others are not saved. Some even use what I've said here to justify their rejection of God. But God is patient, He is waiting and He can wait longer than we can. What He has said still is true. John 5:24 *I tell you the truth, whoever hears my word and believes him who sent me has eternal life and will not be condemned; he has crossed over from death to life.* (NIV®) Regardless of our ability to understand, when we believe in Jesus, we will be saved. We will have jumped off the string onto the bubble even if we can't see it or even understand it.

The Day of the Lord – 2 Peter 3:10

But the day of the Lord will come like a thief, and then the heavens will pass away with a loud noise, and the elements will be dissolved with fire, and the earth and the works that are upon it will be burned up. (RSV)

The "day of the Lord" is a term used in the Bible to denote a time of judgment. We usually think of it as the end of the world, but this is not always the case. When Judah was destroyed and taken into captivity, Jeremiah equated that to the day of the Lord. Lamentations 2:22 *"As you summon to a feast day, so you summoned against me terrors on every side. In the day of the Lord's anger no one escaped or survived; those I cared for and reared, my enemy has destroyed."* (NIV®) One thing is very consistent about the day of the Lord – God is angry and He has had enough. Whether it is a day that has already past or is yet to come, God uses physical destruction to bring judgment on people.

References to the day of the Lord are warnings of what He is going to do in the future. These warnings are for unrepentant sinners so they will repent and turn from the evil He has judged. Isaiah 2:12 *The Lord Almighty has a day in store for all the proud and lofty, for all that is exalted (and they will be humbled).* (NIV®) Isaiah 13:9 *Behold, the day of the Lord comes, cruel, with wrath and fierce anger, to make the earth a desolation and to destroy its sinners from it.* (RSV) The prophet Isaiah used clear and concise words to describe the day of the Lord. Think about it. It is cruel. Cruel means deliberately and remorselessly causing pain or anguish. We seldom think of our loving Heavenly Father as someone who would be cruel, but there it is in black and white. God is going to be cruel; He will demonstrate His wrath and fierce anger. There is no way of getting around this and it should make us wake up and take notice. God's purpose in the destruction of the earth is to destroy sinners. His warnings are provided so that those who heed the warnings will repent and not suffer the wrath that will come.

At some point in time as we know it, God is going to be fed up with sin on the earth and He will no longer be patient. We have no way of knowing when that day will come. It will be like a thief in the night. Jesus warned us in parables to be watching. Luke 12:39-40 *"But understand this: If the owner of the house had known at what hour the thief was coming, he would not have let his house be broken into. You also must be ready, because the Son of Man will come at an hour when you do not expect him."* (NIV®)

What does it mean to be watching? Since His wrath will be against sinners, then the obvious thing a watcher must do is to get out of the "sinner" crowd and into the "holy" crowd. In Matthew 25:1-12 Jesus tells of a parable of ten virgins, five wise and five foolish. What was the distinction between the two groups of virgins or between the "sinner" crowd and the "holy" crowd that the virgins represent? The wise virgins had enough oil to last the night and the foolish didn't. They were prepared; the others were not. The "sinner" crowd isn't prepared because they still cling to their sins. They don't have the oil of the Holy Spirit because they have never repented of their sins and put their faith in Jesus for salvation. They may think they are "spiritual" but they don't have the only spirit that matters, the Holy Spirit.

In the parable, the foolish bang on the door to get in but the bridegroom says he doesn't know them. The "sinner" crowd may even say they know Jesus but their actions show they don't. They had all the time necessary to get prepared, they had the company of the wise virgins and could see that they were prepared, but they put off the decision too long. Just as the bridegroom says he doesn't know the foolish virgins, so Jesus will tell the sinners it is too late on the day of the Lord. They will face the full fury of the Lord.

Just as the wise virgins were given entrance to the wedding supper, so the "holy" crowd will be taken out of the way of God's wrath when it is finally demonstrated. 1 Thessalonians 5:9 *For God did not appoint us to suffer wrath but to receive salvation through our Lord Jesus Christ.* (NIV®) The meaning is very clear. We, who have put our total faith in Jesus for salvation, will not undergo God's wrath. We may have to suffer in many ways, but not due to His wrath.

Go back to the verse in Isaiah and think about His wrath. It is cruel and fierce. When we suffer in this world it is not because God is cruel or angry with us. When God becomes cruel and wrathful against sinners, we don't want to be anywhere near them.

Sometimes we do suffer because we have been associating with sinners or we are simply living in a sinful world. When God brings judgment on others, it causes us pain. When anyone sins, it causes us pain. Even though Jeremiah didn't partake in the sins of Judah, he suffered loss when God judged them.

However, the day of the Lord we are looking forward to is not like the day of the Lord that God brought upon Judah. It is more like the judgment of Korah's rebellion. Numbers 16:23-24 *Then the Lord said to Moses, "Say to the assembly, 'Move away from the tents of Korah, Dathan and Abiram.'"* (NIV®) God calls us to be separate from sinners even when we live in the world. We don't want to be in harm's way when God does judge them.

I think there is going to be at least three more days of the Lord. The first is when Jesus returns for His Bride, the Church. 1 Thessalonians 4:16-17 *For the Lord himself will come down from heaven, with a loud command, with the voice of the archangel and with the trumpet call of God, and the dead in Christ will rise first. After that, we who are still alive and are left will be caught up together with them in the clouds to meet the Lord in the air. And so we will be with the Lord forever.* (NIV®) This is what we call the rapture of the Church. God will separate us from sinners and will then execute judgment on them. Jesus spoke of this in Matthew 24:40-41 and Luke 17:34-35 when He said one will be taken and the other left. At this point, the great tribulation will begin.

During the great tribulation, there will be some people who become Christians and separate themselves from the "sinner" crowd. At the end of the tribulation, there will be another day of the Lord. Again, the Lord will separate sinners from the righteous. Jesus spoke of this time in Matthew 13:37-43 when He explained the parable of the weeds in the field. Matthew 13:41-42 *The Son of Man will send out his angels, and they will weed out of his kingdom everything that causes sin and all who do evil. They will throw them into the fiery furnace, where there will be weeping and gnashing of teeth.* (NIV®) Note the difference between these verses where the wicked are gathered up and tossed in the fire and the verses in 1 Thessalonians

4:16-17 where the righteous are caught up. This second day of the Lord will occur when Jesus comes back in Revelation 19. The separation is also previewed in Revelation 14:14-20 where an angel swings his sickle on the earth to reap a harvest and put it in winepress of God's wrath.

The third day of the Lord will be the very last one and is the one Peter talks about. It is described in Revelation 20:7-21:1. During the millennial reign of Christ, there will be unbelievers. It is hard to imagine that people would not accept Jesus as Lord and Savior when He is physically present on earth. However, there will be billions as is demonstrated at the end. Satan will gather all those who oppose Christ and they will march against Jesus as He reigns in Jerusalem. Poof! Fire from heaven, end of the world, new heaven and new earth. It will be quick and it will be final. It will be the last day of the Lord as believers enter into eternity in the presence of God and unbelievers enter eternity in hell.

I wrote a novel to describe how the events before this last day of the Lord might happen. *999Years After Armageddon – The End of the Millennium.*

Which World Do You Love? – 2 Peter 3:11-13

Since everything around us is going to be destroyed like this, what holy and godly lives you should live, looking forward to the day of God and hurrying it along. On that day, he will set the heavens on fire, and the elements will melt away in the flames. But we are looking forward to the new heavens and new earth he has promised, a world filled with God's righteousness. (NLT)

Peter keeps talking about the destruction of the world. This isn't some flimsy theology based on a couple of obscure passages in the Bible. This is something that each Christian must fully embrace and understand. The earth is temporary. God will completely destroy it and start over with a heaven and earth that will last forever. When we get our minds and hearts around this truth, we can finally live the way He wants us to live. When we are focused on this world and the things of this world, we are ineffective and unproductive in our Christian walk and testimony to the rest of the world.

Paul knew this and it was one of the things that kept him going. After explaining some of the pressures of his ministry, he gave this explanation. 2 Corinthians 4:16-18 *Therefore we do not lose heart. Though outwardly we are wasting away, yet inwardly we are being renewed day by day. For our light and momentary troubles are achieving for us an eternal glory that far outweighs them all. So we fix our eyes not on what is seen, but on what is unseen. For what is seen is temporary, but what is unseen is eternal.* (NIV®) The new heaven and earth are eternal. We don't see them now, but by faith we know they are coming. If we set our eyes on what is happening in this world we can get worked up and frustrated when it appears that our plans or even God's plans are not being accomplished. Either way, rather than obsess with the things of the world, we have to remember that these things are temporary.

Don't get me wrong, however; this doesn't mean we completely ignore the earth or the things in it. In Genesis 2:15, God put Adam in charge of the Garden of Eden to care for it. In Psalm 8:6-8, it says that God has made mankind ruler of all He has made. He does expect us to take good care of the things that He made. In fact, the Bible says that God's wrath is coming on those who destroy the earth. Revelation 11:18 *... Your wrath has come ... for destroying those who destroy the earth.* (NIV®)

The point of Peter and Paul is also emphasized by John. 1 John 2:15-17 *Do not love the world or the things in the world. If any one loves the world, love for the Father is not in him. For all that is in the world, the lust of the flesh and the lust of the eyes and the pride of life, is not of the Father but is of the world. And the world passes away, and the lust of it; but he who does the will of God abides for ever.* (RSV) When John talks about loving the world, he explains that he isn't only talking about the physical things of nature, but also the sinfulness of mankind. This love of the world puts these things above our love of God or of other people. Too much attention to the things of the world violates the greatest commands in the Bible. Matthew 22:37-40 *And he said to him, "You shall love the Lord your God with all your heart, and with all your soul, and with all your mind. This is the great and first commandment. And a second is like it, You shall love your neighbor as yourself. On these two commandments depend all the law and the prophets."* (RSV) God is a jealous God. He wants us to love Him first, people second, and things last. Loving anything more than Him is idolatry.

This is what Peter is trying to get us to understand when he asks what kind of people we ought to be. He says we must live holy and godly lives. The only way to live holy and godly lives is to put God first. To love Him above all things and to love people next. If I love God first then He gives me the power to love others and live a godly life.

How does this speed the day of His coming? It must be tied up in the fact that God desires all to be saved and come to a knowledge of the truth (1 Timothy 2:4). Is it possible that, when the last person whom God has called to salvation actually turns to God, at that time, He will set in motion the events which lead up to the final day of the Lord? If so, then living godly lives and sharing the good news of our salvation through Jesus will hasten the day. If we are lax and don't do our part, then that person may take longer to come to Jesus.

Peter puts a little self-check at the end of this passage. Am I looking forward to this new heaven and earth? Am I looking forward to a world filled with God's righteousness? If not, then why not? Are the goals and desire of this world a higher priority and I don't want to see them destroyed? Do we have goals to get married, see grandchildren grow up, finish college, retire, or any other things that we want more than seeing a world without sin and evil? Many of these goals may be very noble and good, but they can't be more important than seeing the new heaven and earth with God's righteousness filling them.

If I don't want to see Jesus come back because I want any of the things of the world, then my heart is not in the right place. If I truly love Jesus more than anything or anyone else, then I will want to see Him coming back today. I will also understand that this event will far out-shadow anything I might have missed. I will understand that He will take care of all my concerns for others, even those who have not yet made a decision to follow Him.

2 Timothy 4:8 *Now there is in store for me the crown of righteousness, which the Lord, the righteous Judge, will award to me on that day — and not only to me, but also to all who have longed for his appearing.* (NIV®)

Living a Peaceful, Pure and Blameless Life – 2 Peter 3:14

And so, dear friends, while you are waiting for these things to happen, make every effort to be found living peaceful lives that are pure and blameless in his sight. (NLT)

Am I looking forward to the things that Peter mentioned? Am I looking forward to the new heaven and earth? I should be. One of the reasons is that not only will the new heaven and earth be the home of righteousness, but it will also mean that I will see Jesus. Paul tells us we already are citizens of heaven. The Holy Spirit has issued our passport back to our home so it can never be revoked and we should be eagerly waiting for Jesus to come and take us home. When that new universe is created, we will have to be transformed so we can live there and Jesus has the power to change us. Philippians 3:20-21 *But our citizenship is in heaven. And we eagerly await a Savior from there, the Lord Jesus Christ, who, by the power that enables him to bring everything under his control, will transform our lowly bodies so that they will be like his glorious body.* (NIV®)

One thing about that transformed body is that it will never be able to sin. I won't even have to think about resisting temptation or knowing what God's will is. All that is in my current body which causes me to sin will be removed. I don't know about you, but that will be worth the wait. However, we are not there yet. Peter tells us we need to work at living peaceful, pure, and blameless lives right now. We need to make every effort to do this, not just try to do it or work at it sometimes.

One of the key words is effort. It seems a contradiction that we are called to put effort into living holy lives when it is by faith in Jesus' atoning sacrifice that we have been saved. Galatians 3:3 *Are you so foolish? After beginning with the Spirit, are you now trying to attain your goal by human effort?* (NIV®) Paul was trying to show that effort in obedience to the Levitical law, including circumcision, was not going to produce a holy life. The effort we need to exert is in following the Holy Spirit. Galatians 5:16 *So I say, live by the Spirit, and you will not gratify the desires of the sinful nature.* (NIV®)

Paul also describes this effort of living by the Spirit as putting off the old self and putting on the new self. Colossians 3:8-10 *But now*

*you also, put them all aside: anger, wrath, malice, slander, and
abusive speech from your mouth. Do not lie to one another, since you
laid aside the old self with its evil practices, and have put on the new
self who is being renewed to a true knowledge according to the image
of the One who created him.* (NASB) See also Ephesians 4:22-24. The
effort we have to go through is to put aside the sinful habits we once
had when we were not Christians or the habits we have learned from
the world which lead us into sin. The only way to do this is to be
renewed by the Holy Spirit and the way He does this is through the
Word of God and by prayer. 2 Corinthians 5:17 says that we are a
new creation when we become Christians. We need to utilize that new
creation instead of the old self when we respond as Christ would
want.

Renewing our minds takes a couple of things. First of all, we need
to understand what is right and wrong. That's where the Holy Spirit
convicts of right and wrong by the Word of God. We read and
understand that certain things are wrong. For example, we read
Colossians 3:5 *Put to death, therefore, whatever belongs to your
earthly nature: sexual immorality, impurity, lust, evil desires and
greed, which is idolatry.* (NIV®) and Ephesians 4:31-32 *Get rid of all
bitterness, rage and anger, brawling and slander, along with every
form of malice. Be kind and compassionate to one another, forgiving
each other, just as in Christ God forgave you.* (NIV®) We can see the
kinds of behavior that are to be eliminated from our lives and the
behavior that is to replace it.

Then we also need to renew our minds by understanding the
power God gives us to live holy lives. We can't do any putting off and
putting on when we rely only on ourselves. God want us to utilize His
power. Ephesians 1:18-21 *I pray also that the eyes of your heart may
be enlightened in order that you may know the hope to which he has
called you, the riches of his glorious inheritance in the saints, and his
incomparably great power for us who believe. That power is like the
working of his mighty strength, which he exerted in Christ when he
raised him from the dead and seated him at his right hand in the
heavenly realms, far above all rule and authority, power and
dominion, and every title that can be given, not only in the present
age but also in the one to come.* (NIV®) Paul prayed that the
Ephesians would know this power. Note he said that this power is for
us who believe. The very same power that raised Jesus from the grave

and gave Him rule and authority is available to us. Why would we want to rely on our own power to resist evil and live holy lives when we can rely on God's power?

We may have been able to clean up our lives in many areas but we often have a habitual sin that we just can't overcome. We may do well for a while but then fail. We trust Jesus to forgive us (1 John 1:9) and cleanse us from unrighteousness but then the temptation comes again and we succumb. In these situations, you may ask, "How do I rely on His power instead of mine?" That's where prayer comes in. We have to admit to God that we don't have the power in ourselves to resist sin. We've been the ones fighting the temptation and not God.

Hebrews 2:18 *Because he himself suffered when he was tempted, he is able to help those who are being tempted.* (NIV®) What we want is for Jesus to help us and He doesn't until we ask. The next time temptation comes, pray. Tell God you can't do it on your own but you need that same resurrection power to overcome the evil. He will then come to your aid and remove the desire to sin.

You say it still didn't work? Did I mention that you must want to overcome the temptation? If you really want to enjoy that sin then you need to take a step back and ask Him for the power to hate the sin as much as He hates it.

Jesus was tempted in the wilderness by Satan. Each time He was tempted, He used a Scripture to tell Satan why He wouldn't do what Satan wanted. If we don't know God's Word well enough to have a scriptural reason for resisting, then we are in trouble.

James 4:7 *Submit yourselves therefore to God. Resist the devil and he will flee from you.* (RSV) Submitting yourself to God is putting yourself in His hands and trusting His power to overcome the temptation. Resisting the temptation or Satan with Scripture is quoting an appropriate verse when tempted. The temptation may be your own sinful desire or it may come from the devil. It doesn't matter which, because God's Word is more powerful than both.

There is no excuse for failing to overcome habitual sins and making progress in living peaceful lives which are pure and blameless. He has given us the power and the means of appropriating that power. Start living a peaceful, pure, and blameless life today.

God's Patience – 2 Peter 3:15-16

Bear in mind that our Lord's patience means salvation, just as our dear brother Paul also wrote you with the wisdom that God gave him. He writes the same way in all his letters, speaking in them of these matters. His letters contain some things that are hard to understand, which ignorant and unstable people distort, as they do the other Scriptures, to their own destruction. (NIV®)

Back in verse 9 I briefly discussed God's patience which allows more people to be saved. Here, Peter pulls Paul's writings into context. Paul relates some other aspects of God's character in relation to His patience and they also relate to salvation. Romans 2:4 *Or do you presume upon the riches of his kindness and forbearance and patience? Do you not know that God's kindness is meant to lead you to repentance?* (RSV) God's patience is related to His kindness and forbearance or tolerance. His tolerance isn't the politically correct tolerance of the world, but His tolerance is the kind that puts up with something for a while. God puts up with sinful men not to approve of their actions but to give them a chance to repent.

Paul spoke of God's patience for himself. 1 Timothy 1:16 *But for that very reason I was shown mercy so that in me, the worst of sinners, Christ Jesus might display his unlimited patience as an example for those who would believe on him and receive eternal life.* (NIV®) Paul persecuted the church by imprisoning and delivering believers over to execution. You would think that if God was going to destroy anyone, it would have been Paul. However, God had mercy and patience with Paul.

Many Christians today are living ungodly lives. They are living together without marriage. They are idolatrous in the way they handle their finances. They expect political solutions to spiritual problems. They put anything and everything ahead of God in their lives. Many believe that because they are able to keep up the prosperous life, God is OK with their lives. However, the truth is that God is patient with us. He is giving us time to repent. The warning for salvation isn't just for those who don't believe. It is also for believers who are blaspheming the name of Jesus by their lifestyle. He will not always tolerate our way of life.

This isn't anything new. Throughout history, God's people have distorted His Word to suit their own purposes. Jeremiah 22:13-17 *"Woe to him who builds his palace by unrighteousness, his upper rooms by injustice, making his countrymen work for nothing, not paying them for their labor. He says, 'I will build myself a great palace with spacious upper rooms. 'So he makes large windows in it, panels it with cedar and decorates it in red. "Does it make you a king to have more and more cedar? Did not your father have food and drink? He did what was right and just, so all went well with him. He defended the cause of the poor and needy, and so all went well. Is that not what it means to know me?" declares the Lord. "But your eyes and your heart are set only on dishonest gain, on shedding innocent blood and on oppression and extortion."* (NIV®) This is a warning to people of all nations, believers and unbelievers alike. Oppression and extortion can take many forms. It can be as simple as not sharing with others in need, taking advantage of illegal aliens or blatant slavery. It can be looking for legal loopholes to do unethical business practices. What about those houses? I'm sure the rich have every right to build million dollar mansions, but do they do that to the exclusion of sharing their wealth?

An interesting aspect of this passage is Peter's reference to Paul's writings. If there is ever any question about the authority of Paul's writings and his apostleship, this should clear it up. Peter affirms Paul as a dear brother. This is in spite of the fact that Paul had to call Peter to account for his unbiblical behavior. Galatians 2:11 *When Peter came to Antioch, I opposed him to his face, because he was clearly in the wrong.* (NIV®) Next, Peter affirms that what Paul wrote was through the wisdom God gave him. The third interesting thing is that Peter equates Paul's writing with Scripture. Up until this time, the only writing that was held in this high esteem was what we would now call the Old Testament – or the Jewish Bible. Even though Paul was not counted with the original Apostles, Peter recognized that God had used him to teach us through his writings. Paul's letters are now universally accepted as God's Word.

Peter also affirms that Paul's writings aren't always easy to understand. However, difficulty in understanding doesn't give anyone an excuse to distort what he wrote. The warning against this is clear. Anyone who distorts the Bible will bring destruction upon themselves. I have to be careful what I say when I talk or write about the Bible. Each preacher needs to be careful. Any application of Scripture to everyday life must be correct, leading to righteousness, holiness, salvation, kindness, perseverance, all the fruit of the Spirit. Using any Scripture to justify ungodly behavior will only result in heartache, sin, and possible destruction. Don't be ignorant and unstable.

Stability – 2 Peter 3:17-18

You therefore, beloved, knowing this beforehand, beware lest you be carried away with the error of lawless men and lose your own stability. But grow in the grace and knowledge of our Lord and Savior Jesus Christ. To him be the glory both now and to the day of eternity. Amen. (RSV)

There are charismatic Bible teachers, who by persuasive words and even deceptive demonstrations of what they call the power of the Holy Spirit, lead people into error. There are others who repeat the error often enough until it finally sounds like the truth. Peter taught us many things in this epistle so this should not happen.

In chapter one, Peter taught us that God has already given us everything we need to escape the corruption in the world and to live godly lives. He has affirmed that we are partakers of the divine nature – we have His Holy Spirit living in us. But we also need to make an effort to develop the fruit of the Holy Spirit in our lives. If we don't, we forget about our salvation and our lives are unproductive.

Peter also taught us about the certainty of the Scriptures. Unlike the teaching of false prophets, God's Word, the Bible, is a product of the Holy Spirit working through the men He chose. Peter affirms his own eyewitness account of Jesus. He supports Paul and his letters as an apostle speaking with the same authority as the rest of Scripture.

He warns us about false teachers and how to identify them by their life style. In doing this, he also warns us about the judgment that will come upon the false teachers. If we are ever inclined to utter prophecies or teach, then we had better be careful, as that same judgment will come upon us if we are doing this by our own power and not by the Holy Spirit.

What is even scarier is that Peter calls into question whether or not these people have ever been saved. These warnings are scattered throughout the book as he asks us to make sure of our own calling and talks about those who become entangled again in the corruption of the world after having had only head knowledge of Jesus. Eternal security only applies to those who have truly surrendered their lives to Jesus.

Peter reminds us of God's patience and the judgment that awaits those who spurn His patience and kindness. While we wait for the final destruction of the heavens and earth, Peter calls us to live holy lives. Living as God wants us to will actually bring that day sooner. I suspect that some may want to live godless lives so the day will not come as soon. But even in that case, God is sovereign and His plan will not be thwarted.

If we don't hang on to the things about which Peter has reminded us, then we can become unstable. It isn't surprising that counseling offices are filled with people who need these reminders. Jesus has been called The Rock. That is because He is stable. When we are firmly fixed on The Rock, we will also be stable. When we are carried away by error or our own sinful desires, we slip from The Rock and the warnings of Peter become manifested in our lives.

Peter's final words are a command to grow in the grace and knowledge of Jesus. That is the way to stay stable in our Christian walk.

Appendix I – Resurrection Proof

If someone were to tell you he didn't believe that Jesus died on the cross, but rather He had been alive and later walked out of the tomb, how would you answer him? How would you answer someone who said He had died, but that the disciples had stolen the body? Can you prove from the Scriptures that Jesus did die on the cross and was raised? The Word is all we need to use because it reflects the viewpoint of several witnesses, which is what would be needed in a court of law. The witnesses don't reflect exactly the same wording; this shows that there wasn't a conspiracy to propagate a concocted story.

Proof that Jesus died:

John 19:31-34 *Now it was the day of Preparation, and the next day was to be a special Sabbath. Because the Jews did not want the bodies left on the crosses during the Sabbath, they asked Pilate to have the legs broken and the bodies taken down. The soldiers therefore came and broke the legs of the first man who had been crucified with Jesus, and then those of the other. But when they came to Jesus and found that he was already dead, they did not break his legs. Instead, one of the soldiers pierced Jesus' side with a spear, bringing a sudden flow of blood and water.* (NIV®) The Roman soldiers were experts in making sure someone was dead. That's why they broke the leg bones of the two criminals. With broken legs, they wouldn't be able to support themselves and they would suffocate. When they pierced Jesus with the spear, blood and water flowed out. Any physician can tell you that this was a sure sign of death since blood immediately separates into serum (water) and blood cells at death.

John 19:38-40 *Later, Joseph of Arimathea asked Pilate for the body of Jesus. Now Joseph was a disciple of Jesus, but secretly because he feared the Jews. With Pilate's permission, he came and took the body away. He was accompanied by Nicodemus, the man who earlier had visited Jesus at night. Nicodemus brought a mixture of myrrh and aloes, about seventy-five pounds. Taking Jesus' body, the two of them wrapped it, with the spices, in strips of linen. This was in accordance with Jewish burial customs.* (NIV®) Even if Jesus hadn't died on the cross, this process of wrapping in Him beneath multiple layers of linen and spice (75 pounds) would have probably killed Him because of His weakened condition after His scourging. Do you think that these two men would have continued to wrap Him if He had shown any signs of life?

Mark 15:43-45 *Joseph of Arimathea, a prominent member of the Council, who was himself waiting for the kingdom of God, went boldly to Pilate and asked for Jesus' body. Pilate was surprised to hear that he was already dead. Summoning the centurion, he asked him if Jesus had already died. When he learned from the centurion that it was so, he gave the body to Joseph.* (NIV®) Pilate gave his permission to give the body of Jesus to Joseph only after he had the word of the centurion that he was dead. This Roman governor and the centurion were essentially staking their lives on the fact that Jesus was dead.

Proof that the disciples didn't steal the body:

Matthew 27:63-66 *"Sir," they said, "we remember that while he was still alive that deceiver said, 'After three days I will rise again.' So give the order for the tomb to be made secure until the third day. Otherwise, his disciples may come and steal the body and tell the people that he has been raised from the dead. This last deception will be worse than the first." "Take a guard," Pilate answered. "Go, make the tomb as secure as you know how." So they went and made the tomb secure by putting a seal on the stone and posting the guard.* (NIV®) A Roman guard was put on watch to make sure that no one entered or left the tomb. There would probably be at least four trained soldiers at any time. The penalty that they would face for messing up on the job was death. If the disciples tried to steal the body, they would have been in for fight and the Romans would have to be killed or seriously injured to get the body. Take a look at the account of the disciples in the garden when Jesus was captured. Peter wasn't an accomplished swordsman. The disciples would also have been wanted men and would not have been able to move about publicly as they did after Pentecost.

Matthew 28:2-4 *There was a violent earthquake, for an angel of the Lord came down from heaven and, going to the tomb, rolled back the stone and sat on it. His appearance was like lightning, and his clothes were white as snow. The guards were so afraid of him that they shook and became like dead men.* (NIV®) There was more than one guard, which supports the history books' descriptions of the Roman guards. They were frightened to death by the angel. With God's intervention in this manner, there is no doubt that the disciples didn't have to do anything to fake a resurrection.

Matthew 28:11-15 *While the women were on their way, some of the guards went into the city and reported to the chief priests everything that had happened. When the chief priests had met with the elders and devised a plan, they gave the soldiers a large sum of money, telling them, "You are to say, 'His disciples came during the night and stole him away while we were asleep.' If this report gets to the governor, we will satisfy him and keep you out of trouble." So the soldiers took the money and did as they were instructed. And this story has been widely circulated among the Jews to this very day.* (NIV®) This account explains why people claim the disciples stole the body. What this really shows is that the chief priests had to pay the governor as well as the soldiers to tell the story. If the governor had not been bought off, the guards would have lost their lives for losing the body. The guards had to be bought off because they were essentially out of work and disgraced for having "fallen asleep" while on guard duty.

Mark 15:47 *Mary Magdalene and Mary the mother of Joses saw where he was laid.* (NIV®) Just in case someone may say that the women and the disciples went to the wrong tomb, this verse lets us know His burial was done in full view of many witnesses. Besides that, the officials would have simply produced the body and settled the matter.

John 20:5-8 *He bent over and looked in at the strips of linen lying there but did not go in. Then Simon Peter, who was behind him, arrived and went into the tomb. He saw the strips of linen lying there,*

as well as the burial cloth that had been around Jesus' head. The
cloth was folded up by itself, separate from the linen. Finally the
other disciple, who had reached the tomb first, also went inside. He
saw and believed.* (NIV®) There are two things here that verify the
resurrection and the fact that the disciples didn't steal the body. These
involve the description of the strips of linen and the folded head cloth.
They were lying there. If you were going to snatch a body from under
Roman guard in the middle of the night, would you take the time to
unwrap the body or fold the head cloth? The other thing is the use of
the word that describes the strips of linen. It is the Greek word
"keimai" which means – 1) to lie. a) used of an infant b) used of one
buried c) used of things that quietly cover some spot; for example, a
city situated on a hill d) used of things put or set in any place, in
reference to which we often use "to stand": of vessels, of a throne, of
the site of a city, of grain and other things laid up together, of a
foundation. The way others and I look at this definition is it implies
the strips were vacated without having been unwrapped. They were
still set in place and collapsed on the spot where Jesus had been.
John's response when he saw this was profound – he believed. By the
way, this is one of the reasons why I don't buy the theory that the
Shroud of Turin is Jesus' burial cloth. They used strips of linen and
had it interwoven with spices; they didn't use a single cloth. There
was also a separate head cloth.

We also have the witness of the disciples and the women. These are
the most well known witnesses and I won't quote all the verses
regarding their encounters with the resurrected Christ. However,
many more saw Jesus after the resurrection. 1 Corinthians 15:3-8 *For
what I received I passed on to you as of first importance: that Christ
died for our sins according to the Scriptures, that he was buried, that
he was raised on the third day according to the Scriptures, and that
he appeared to Peter, and then to the Twelve. After that, he appeared
to more than five hundred of the brothers at the same time, most of
whom are still living, though some have fallen asleep. Then he
appeared to James, then to all the apostles, and last of all he
appeared to me also, as to one abnormally born.* (NIV®) At the time
Paul wrote this, there were hundreds of people who had seen Jesus
alive after the resurrection. Anyone could interview them and verify

the fact that Jesus had risen. In a court of law, there is a preponderance of proof that Jesus died and was resurrected.

Paul was so sure Jesus was raised that he rightfully declared His resurrection is the proof of Christianity. 1 Corinthians 15:12-19 *But if it is preached that Christ has been raised from the dead, how can some of you say that there is no resurrection of the dead? If there is no resurrection of the dead, then not even Christ has been raised. And if Christ has not been raised, our preaching is useless and so is your faith. More than that, we are then found to be false witnesses about God, for we have testified about God that he raised Christ from the dead. But he did not raise him if in fact the dead are not raised. For if the dead are not raised, then Christ has not been raised either. And if Christ has not been raised, your faith is futile; you are still in your sins. Then those also who have fallen asleep in Christ are lost. If only for this life we have hope in Christ, we are to be pitied more than all men.* (NIV®) Jesus' resurrection proves that He is who He said He was. It is proof that His death on the cross is sufficient to pay for our sins. If Jesus had not been raised from the dead, then we would be fools to follow Him today. Since He has been raised, we are fools if we don't place our faith in Him for the forgiveness of our sins and our eternal salvation, as well as our hope for this life.

Appendix II – Study Questions

I provided the questions in this appendix for either group or individual study. I addressed many of the questions in length in this book; however, I did not answer all of them directly or in the same order as asked here.

My reflections on 1st and 2nd Peter as well as any other person's comments are fallible but the Word of God is not. I pray that the Bible becomes your first and best source of answers to these and all questions. I have found that the best way to answer my own questions is to prayerfully search the Bible and let the Holy Spirit guide me.

Finally, when I study God's Word, it must result in a response that pleases God. If it doesn't help me overcome sin, trust Jesus more, and become more like Jesus, then it is only head knowledge that will only turn me in to a Pharisee. As you answer these questions, I pray that you also will ask yourself, "So what am I to do in response?"

1 Peter 1:1-6
1. What does it mean to be God's elect – chosen in Him?
2. How are we strangers in the world? What does that look like when we interact with each other, Christians or non-Christians?
3. How does the Holy Spirit sanctify us?
4. What does it mean to be sprinkled by Jesus' blood?
5. How do we bless, praise, or worship God in everyday life?
6. What does it mean to be born again? Where else is this terminology used in Scripture?
7. What is the living hope that we have?
8. Describe our inheritance. What is it, where is it, how is it kept safe?
9. Aren't believers already saved? What is this salvation that will be revealed in the last times?

1 Peter 1:7-12
1. What do we need to focus on to get through trials?
2. What is the purpose of these trials?
3. Do you love Jesus? How does that love make a difference in your life?

4. What is the grace that has come to us about which the Old Testament prophets spoke?
5. What verses can you find in the Old Testament which point to the grace that has come to us?
6. What verses can you find in the Old Testament that foretold Jesus' suffering?
7. What are the glories that are yet to be revealed?

1 Peter 1:13-25

1. How can you prepare your mind for action?
2. How does setting your mind on the grace to be given help you be obedient?
3. What are some of the evil desire you used to have in the past? Have you overcome them?
4. How does examining God's holiness help us to be holy?
5. What does it mean to live in reverent fear of God and why should we?
6. What are some of the empty ways in which people try to earn God's favor?
7. What does it mean to be redeemed? What are we redeemed from?
8. What Old Testament passages relate to redemption?
9. How is it possible that Christ's blood could redeem us?
10. How was Jesus chosen before the creation of the world?
11. Why was Jesus revealed and what does that mean?
12. Is it possible to believe in God without Jesus?
13. If the Holy Spirit is the one who sanctifies us, how do we purify ourselves?
14. What is a result of purifying yourself? Have you done this? Do you see the results in your life?
15. What is the imperishable seed that gives us new birth?
16. How has the Word of God shown itself to be everlasting?

1 Peter 2:1-10

1. How is it possible to get rid of the sins listed in 1 Peter 2:1?
2. What is spiritual milk? Where else in Scripture is this referenced?
3. What does it mean to taste that the Lord is good?

4. When you read that we are living stones of a spiritual house, what does that mean?
5. Who are members of the holy priesthood?
6. What are spiritual sacrifices that are acceptable to God?
7. Have you ever been ashamed of your faith? Why?
8. Why should a person who trusts in Jesus never be ashamed?
9. How is Jesus a stumbling block to those who don't believe in Him?
10. What will be the result of those who stumble over Jesus?
11. Why can't we write off someone who doesn't believe in Jesus? Aren't they destined for disobedience?
12. If we are chosen and some are destined to disobey, why should we preach the Gospel? Won't all who are destined for salvation be saved?
13. Do you remember when you were not part of God's people? What was your attitude toward God?
14. How has that attitude changed and why has it changed?

1 Peter 2:11-25
1. How is it possible to abstain from sinful desires? How can you win that war against your soul?
2. What should be the result of living as aliens and strangers in this world who do abstain from evil desires?
3. Will those who try to discredit Christians be able to see your good deeds or does your behavior fuel their criticism?
4. Do you submit to the laws of the land and the authority of our leaders?
5. What is the purpose of the governing authorities?
6. When might it be all right to disobey the laws?
7. How can your behavior toward the government silence the talk of foolish people and how can it incite them?
8. How can Christians bring discredit on themselves with regard to their work and their employers?
9. What is the example Jesus provided that we can apply to our work and daily lives?
10. How do you react when someone insults you? Do you retaliate? Do you let your righteous life speak for you?
11. How could Jesus bear our sins?

12. How do you die to sin? Have you let Jesus' wounds heal your sinful nature?

1 Peter 3:1-7

1. What does it mean for a woman to be submissive to her husband? Does this apply whether or not the husband is a Christian?
2. What reason does Peter give a woman to be submissive?
3. What is the correlation between being pure and reverent to winning an unbelieving husband? Does this apply only to women?
4. Does Peter prohibit women from braiding their hair or wearing jewelry?
5. What is the attitude that a woman should have to please God? Does this apply only to women?
6. Explain how Sarah obeyed Abraham and the benefits received, as well as times when she didn't demonstrate trust in God and the consequences of her actions.
7. How can being fearful sidetrack you from living as God wants you?
8. Why do you think that a husband treating his wife incorrectly will have his prayers hindered?
9. What does Peter mean when he says that a wife is a weaker vessel?

1 Peter 3:8-17

1. If everyone were to follow the command in 1 Peter 3:8-9, do you think the previous instructions to husbands and wives would be necessary? Why or why not?
2. List the three areas where we need to be careful in order to love life and see good days.
3. Do you feel like your prayer life is less than it should be? Examine your life in view of 1 Peter 3:1-11. What things do you need to do differently so that God will be attentive to your prayers?
4. What is the remedy for fearing to do what is good?
5. Are you prepared to give the reason for the hope that you have? Take time to write out what you would say if asked.
6. What attitudes should you have as you present your hope?

7. Why do your actions sometimes speak louder than words? What will happen if your actions and words don't agree?

1 Peter 3:18-22
1. Is there any sin that Jesus didn't die for? Is there any person that Jesus didn't die for?
2. Why did Jesus die?
3. How could Jesus, who is God, die and then be resurrected?
4. How was Jesus able to preach to spirits in prison?
5. Who are those spirits in prison and why are they there?
6. How is the flood of Noah's time related to baptism?
7. How or why does baptism save a person?
8. If a person claims to be a Christian, does not demonstrate a life of repentance, but gets baptized, is he saved? Why or why not?
9. If a person claims to be a Christian, demonstrates a life of repentance, but does not get baptized, is he saved? Why or why not?
10. What does Jesus' resurrection prove?

1 Peter 4:1-6
1. What kind of attitude do we need about suffering and why?
2. Explain whether or not you will ever be completely done with sin.
3. What is required to be free from sin?
4. Have you had a sinful past? If so, how did your friends react when you gave up your past behavior?
5. What will happen to those who abuse others because they want to do what is right?
6. Does 1 Peter 4:6 mean there is always a second chance after death for people to become Christians? Explain why you answered as you did.

1 Peter 4:7-11
1. Do you believe the end of all things is near? How does your answer affect your attitude in living for Christ and praying?
2. How does love cover over a multitude of sins?

3. What is the effect (spiritually and physically) of offering hospitality and grumbling about it? How does this apply to other aspects of Christian service?
4. Where do we get our abilities to serve? How should this affect the way we serve?
5. Who should get the credit for our service?

1 Peter 4:12-19

1. Why shouldn't we be surprised when we undergo suffering?
2. In what circumstances can we be blessed when we suffer?
3. In what circumstances will we not be blessed when we suffer?
4. Are you ashamed to be called a Christian? Are you afraid that it will cause suffering or ridicule? What should your attitude be?
5. What did Peter mean or imply regarding suffering and judgment beginning with the family of God?
6. If God's family is judged and suffer, what will be the outcome be for those who are not part of His family?
7. If you find yourself suffering, what things do you need to change? What is the one thing you should not change?

1 Peter 5:1-6

1. How does Peter identify himself?
2. What is the primary motivation and attitude that a shepherd must have?
3. How can a shepherd know if he is called to be a shepherd?
4. What is the ultimate reward a shepherd will receive?
5. In what way are young men to be submissive to those who are older?
6. Discussing younger and older, shepherds and the flock, who should be showing humility to whom?
7. What is the reason to have humility toward others? What are the results if you don't and if you do?

1 Peter 5:7-14

1. How do you cast your anxieties on God?
2. What is the relationship between anxieties and Satan?
3. What four things can you do to resist Satan?

4. How does knowing that others are undergoing suffering help you resist Satan?
5. Explain what you think the eternal glories in Christ will be like.
6. How does knowing your eternal calling help you bear up under suffering? Or does it?
7. How does God restore you? Have you experienced this in your life? If so, have you shared it with others?
8. What kind of power does God have in your life?
9. What is the true grace of God?
10. Who do you think is "she who is in Babylon?"
11. What kind of peace do you have in Christ?

2 Peter 1:1-4

1. How would you describe an apostle of Jesus?
2. Do you have a problem with calling Jesus God and Savior? (Verse one calls Jesus God and Savior, verse two appears to make a distinction between the two.) How do you explain the Trinity?
3. Explain how we receive faith.
4. Have you ever considered how precious your faith is? Write down what your faith means to you.
5. Explain how you have experienced grace and peace in abundance through Jesus Christ.
6. Can you think of any area in your life where you have lacked for life and godliness? If so, why do you think you have lacked it? If not, share with others how God has provided.
7. What has God called you to and by what means has He called you?
8. Take some time to write down God's promises to us.

2 Peter 1:4-9

1. What do you think it means to participate in God's divine nature?
2. What happens when we participate in His nature?

3. Why do you suppose it takes effort to add the qualities listed in verses five and six to our faith?
4. Take time to evaluate each of these qualities in your own life. Where are you lacking? What do you need to do to add them to your faith and strengthen them?
5. Describe an effective and productive life.
6. How would you rate your knowledge of Jesus when you consider that it should be effective and productive in living your life?
7. What is one of the biggest reasons someone might not be developing these qualities?

2 Peter 1:10-21

1. Why do you think Peter tells us to make our calling and election sure? Is it possible to be reading this book and working on these questions and not be called by God or elected?
2. Take some time and write down what you expect may happen when you enter the eternal kingdom.
3. Why do we always need to be reminded of our faith and biblical principles?
4. Why is it important for us to remind others about the same things?
5. Do you look forward to your departure from this life and entering eternity? Why or why not?
6. How can you distinguish between myths, cleverly invented stories, and biblical truth?
7. What does Peter mean when he speaks of the morning star rising in our hearts?
8. What has made the word of the prophets more certain?
9. What is the source of all prophecy and Scripture?

2 Peter 2:1-9

1. Can you identify any false prophets who are in the Bible?
2. What happens to those who introduce heresies?
3. Can you identify some of the ways current false teaching denies Jesus?
4. What are some of the ways you can identify a false teacher?
5. What is the condemnation that will occur for false teachers?

6. Consider the destruction by the flood and of Sodom and Gomorrah. What do you learn from these examples?
7. What is the deliverance that is promised to righteous people who undergo trials?

2 Peter 2:10-22

1. What are some of the blatant sins of those who will be punished in the judgment?
2. List the different kinds of celestial beings. How should we act in regard to them?
3. Think about the many descriptive words used to describe false teachers. Do any of them apply to you? Have you wandered into any of these areas?
4. Have you been influenced by books or teachers who are very clever in their writing or speech but actually appeal to your sinful nature? How would you know if it did happen? How can you prevent it from happening?
5. Have you recently escaped from error? Why may you be more vulnerable than others to false teaching?
6. Is it possible for a person to be a true Christian and then return to a life of sin? Explain and support your argument from Scripture.
7. Is it possible for a person to clean up his life by living according to the Christian faith and still not be a Christian? If so, what is his eventual destiny?

2 Peter 3:1-9

1. What is a purpose of the Bible as described here? How is this accomplished?
2. Why do some people (scoffers) make fun of the Bible?
3. What are some of the ways they ridicule the Bible as listed here and any other ways you have observed?
4. God's Word has accomplished two things in the past and will do one more thing. What are they?
5. Why do you think people choose to forget that God created the world?
6. What is the eventual end of the world and what will be the fate of ungodly people at that time?
7. Why does God's fulfillment of promises seem slow to us?

8. Why doesn't God destroy the earth now and get rid of all sin?

2 Peter 3:10-18
1. Describe what you think it will look like when the earth is destroyed. Are there other Bible verses where this is described that will help you?
2. How can we know when these things will occur?
3. As you think about the eventual destruction of the earth and judgment, how does that change the way you live?
4. Are you looking forward to a new heaven and earth? Why or why not? What is keeping you from that?
5. How does Peter confirm that all of Paul's writings belong in the Bible?
6. When someone distorts or changes what the Bible says, what will happen to them?
7. What do you need to be on guard against?
8. What do you need to do to keep from falling into sin and following evil men

Other Books by Ray Ruppert

Novels

999 Years After Armageddon: The End of the Millennium

Have you ever wondered why anyone would want to try to defeat Jesus Christ after He has been ruling on the earth for a thousand years? Have you wondered how Satan can deceive billions of people while Jesus is physically present on the earth? Do you wonder how people will rule with Christ and govern the nations with a rod of iron? In this novel, you will find the answer to these and many other questions about life 999 years after the battle of Armageddon in this new world order called the Millennium Reign of Christ.

Those who oppose the new world order will make you wonder if the world ruler, The Sovereign Yehowshuwa, is really who he claims to be. They uncover knowledge hidden for ages and present compelling arguments to prove the wrong person won the battle of Armageddon. Was humanity's real savior, The Chancellor Ben-Shaachar, imprisoned for one thousand years?

Originally presented in two books, The Sovereign Reigns, or Does He? and The Sovereign's Last Battle, 999 Years After Armageddon – The End of the Millennium contains the complete story for your reading enjoyment.

The Voice of Con

Con artists Darryl Smith and his girlfriend Renee Cleve have the perfect scam helping Vietnam era draftees escape military service by enabling them to fail their physical and get a 4-F status. Darryl is aided by a voice that speaks to him, providing guidance and the power to manipulate others.

Their newest "client" is very wealthy and provides the temptation to get more than their usual pay for their draft dodging services. Instead of being on easy street they find themselves in over their heads as they come up against the mob.

Education

Battling Satan with the Armor of God

Our worst enemy is Satan and it is no joke that he is seeking to devour us (1 Peter 5:8). We need to know our enemy or we will always be on the defensive and we will suffer defeat. We can't live a victorious Christian life if we underestimate Satan's power and abilities. We are told to take our stand against the devil's schemes (Ephesians 6:11).

This booklet will help us understand Satan's abilities and the spiritual realm in which he operates. It looks at the cosmic battle that has been waging since the beginning of time, Satan's origins, his fall, powers of heavenly beings, and more.

Knowing these things will help us understand Satan's capabilities so that we can use the armor of God to overcome his schemes and live a victorious Christian life.

Books for Kids

Cows for Kids Cow Fun and Facts

Written by Malinda Mitchell, Photography by Ray Ruppert - Cows for Kids, Cow Fun and Facts, is a fun filled learning experience about cattle. It's chock-full of beautiful photos of various breeds, colors, sizes, and ages of cattle. It's fun because you can tell what the cows are thinking! They have quite a sense of humor. It's educational as facts are interspersed with the fun.

Dairy cows are featured with actual photos of cows lining up to get milked and the actual milking operation. It is udderly fascinating and educational!

Since calves are so cute, there is an abundance of pictures of calves ranging from newborn to several weeks old. You'll learn what it takes for a newborn calf to be healthy.

You will also get to see young people grooming and preparing their animals for show. These 4-H and FFA youngsters are learning what it takes to care for and even breed cattle. When show time comes you can see the results.

The last section of this book shows how Werkoven Dairy and Qualco Energy have teamed up to provide an environmentally friendly farm that uses the manure to benefit farmers, fishermen, and families. "This book is a great learning tool." — Qualco Energy Board of directors

For added enjoyment, a fun quiz is at the end of the book. Be careful, there may be some trick questions.

Malinda is an accomplished author of many children's books. She lives in Mississippi. Ray Ruppert lives in western Washington where most of these pictures were taken. This is the second book that Malinda Mitchell and Ray Ruppert have produced together.

Respect and Enjoy God's Creation

Written by Malinda Mitchell, Photography by Ray Ruppert - God's creation is all around us. Malinda Mitchell provides great tips for children to learn how to respect His creation. Whether on vacation, visiting a farm, zoo, or just in their own back yard, children will be able to appreciate and learn more about the way we have been blessed with God's creation.

Each page is accompanied by photographs which will inspire children and adults alike.

You will want to get this book and read it to your younger children or have your older ones read it to you. You can discuss how God has provided for us through His creation and how we should take good care of what He has provided.

Malinda Mitchell resides in Mississippi with her husband, Alton. She has four grown children, a seventeen-year-old son, and eight grandchildren. Malinda has been writing fiction for all ages for more than forty years. Malinda's favorite interests are spending time with family and friends, writing, and still-life oil painting. Malinda also had articles published in the 2008 summer and 2009 spring issues of Once Upon A Time Magazine before they closed their doors. She also writes for a card company.

Ray Ruppert is an amateur photographer, and author. He lives in Washington State with his wife, Terri, where many of the pictures in this book were taken. The cover photo is of the Skykomish valley as seen from Wallace Falls.

www.ingramcontent.com/pod-product-compliance
Lightning Source LLC
Chambersburg PA
CBHW071532040426
42452CB00008B/989